It Isn't All Greek To Me

By the same author

To Sea in a Sieve
Bulls in the Meadows
I Know the Face, But . . .
Not on your Telly!
I Say, Look Here!

PETER BULL

It Isn't All Greek To Me

Illustrations by Roger Furse

Noverre Press

First published in 1967
© 1967 Peter Bull

This edition published in 2016 by
The Noverre Press
Southwold House
Isington Road
Binsted
Hampshire
GU34 4PH

ISBN 978-1-906830-75-5

© 2016 The Noverre Press

Contents

Page

Illustrations

Page

For Nikos Kaloudis
with love and gratitude

1. *Nikos the Fisherman*

It all began with Nikos the Fisherman or 'fissesman' as he would pronounce the word. And I want to make it quite clear from the outset that if I were contributing to the *Reader's Digest* in that section devoted to 'The Most Unforgettable Character I Have Ever Met' my choice would automatically be Nikos the F.

I have long ago given up being surprised by anything that happens to me but I am pretty certain that I would have laughed in anyone's face (Ha! Ha! HA!) if they'd told me that my entire life was going to be changed by a forty-five-year-old Corfiote, for that is what an inhabitant of the Ionian island of Corfu is called.

The chain of events leading up to my coming across Nikos was bizarre enough in itself. Before I became the great Greek Bore, as you are going to find out to your cost, I had been the great Spanish Bore, with my Spanish lisp, the gerahe (garage), potht offith (post office) type conversation and the bullfighting posters in my hathienda (flat in the King's Road, Chelsea). For longish periods annually I had been going to a small village in the south of Spain for peace, sun, sea and a little writing-producing boredom. But suddenly, overnight it seemed, the idyllic spot that I had selected for my self-indulgence was seized on for development and became an international zone of bedlam, self-service stores and indeed self-service ladies and gentlemen. The streets were strewn with expatriates from all over the world and the usual plasma of alcoholics, drug-fiends and Students of Life littered the bars and confused everyone.

My little Utopia vanished in front of my eyes and, to cap it all, my ill-advised and I suppose bossy interference in somebody else's life had resulted in the arrival of an unbalanced female at a small pensione which up till then I had looked on as completely free from other foreign bodies. This particular f.b. was convinced that I wished to spend the rest of my time on earth with her. It was an incorrect assumption and I had tried on numerous occasions to persuade her to abandon it. But reasonable and factual thinking was not in her make-up and her whole attitude was theatrical in the extreme. She had just obtained a divorce from her husband. 'I managed to keep your name out of it', she reported to me obligingly and I didn't have the heart to tell her that two meetings, one in the glove dept of Derry and Toms and the other in a with-it café in downtown Kensington, wouldn't necessarily imply that I had committed adultery with her.

But the whole dotty business had finally got on my wick and I decided to press on from the Costa del Sol. I had always had a faint but lazy inclination to go to the Isles of Greece where dear old Sappho seemed to find plenty of inspiration and heaven knows I needed that. The trouble with finding a 'Work with Play' environment is that one would prefer a totally primitive and almost boringly beautiful spot with just one oasis within speaking and visiting distance. Otherwise one goes barking unless one is v. strong-minded and disciplined. I knew nobody in the whole of Greece, apart from an acquaintance in the island of

Hydra, and practically nothing about the country itself. I of course knew that 'Hoi Polloi' was a snobby way to describe the Common People and that people kept popping into horses made of wood.

So I thought I'd better start at the heart of things and get Athens and the dear old Akropolis and all that Over. I must confess with genuine shame my total inability to absorb any form of culture and I don't even know What I Like, because it alters all the time, 'What I Like', I mean. Being a mine of absolutely Useless Information it is impossible to fill my head with even a surface layer of erudition, and a mere glimpse of the Pyramids from a distance is sufficient to send me scurrying back to the bazaars of Cairo on the nearest camel. My list of famous places I have never visited, even though in the area, is a formidable one and I shan't humiliate myself further by naming them.

But in this case it was impossible to avoid the Akrop and the Parthenon and v. nice they looked. Even I saw that. But it was terribly hot in the Greek capital and I wanted to get into that sea like Miss Melina Mercouri did in the opening sequence of *Never on Sonntag*. Except that if I'd dived in where she did I would undoubtedly have caught typhoid. The harbour of the Piraeus has never been classed as one of the best swimming areas in the Mediterranean, and I decided to visit Hydra. It is absolutely beautiful but at the time of my brief sojourn it was full of Students of Life from England and America who could have found out most of the info for which they were searching in an evening on the King's Road or Forty-Second Street. In fact it was very little different, atmosphere-wise, from what I had just escaped in Spain. So I pressed on to the other islands of the group—Poros, Aegina and Spetsai. But even there I found signs of development and, apart from a merciful absence of Coca-Cola advertisements, all the other portents of emerging 'civilization', question mark, were present. Hopefully I sped across Greece in a high-powered bus and ended up in Albert Finney's villa in Corfu. You heard! You haven't got cloth ears! Albert Finney's villa in Corfu.

For some months previous to my drastic change of direction

I had been appearing with this not totally untalented young gent in a play by John Osborne about M. Luther, and the night I gave him the news of my evacuation to Greece he retaliated rather haughtily by asking what was so special about that pronunciamento. He himself had that morning rented a mansion in Corfu on the outskirts of the capital and he might be able to squeeze me in if I'd like it. I said snap yes indeedy and that I would clock in on Good Friday (Greek) if that'd suit. I was showing off (as usual) as I knew that Greece was a week behind us that partic year in the celebration of Easter and I didn't want there to be a misunderstanding.

And I'm jolly glad there wasn't one because my first Easter in Corfu was unforgettable. It is a very special occasion there and far exceeds Christmas in both expectation and fulfilment. Its significance seems to be more generally and deeply felt than in other countries and the traditional observances are deeply impressive. Some of the near-pagan, or so they seem to us, aspects remain and I do find the mass slaughtering of lambs with the attendant smearing of blood on doorways etc. deeply alarming. It is particularly disturbing to find that animals which have been cosseted, loved and treated as one of the family should meet with a slightly more violent death than the usual one.

Strict fasting is maintained through Great Week (Holy ditto) and, though the tourist is adequately catered for over this period, restaurants and cafés are little frequented by Corfiotes. In Corfu the excitement is intense and certain rituals are carried out which do not take place elsewhere in Greece.

The festival is dominated by the spirit and actual presence (in embalmed person) of the patron saint of the island, St Spiridion, who is carted round the town, tiny in a bejewelled casket. His little head is propped up at the side and the faithful can kiss his slippered feet before he returns to rest in the church bearing his name. For exceptionally droll information about feet kissing and other Corfiot rituals see *My Family and Other Animals* by Gerald Durrell and for a riveting biography of the saint himself see his brother's exquisite tribute to Corfu, entitled *Prospero's Cell*. Oh

4

lawks! I wish I hadn't mentioned them two so early on. It gives me a vast inferiority complex.

However press on, that's what I always say, which makes any conversation with me so boring. And that's exactly what I did from Athens to Corfu. By a bus as a matter of fact, which starts off at four-thirty in the morning. It was crammed with Corfiotes returning from the capital for the Easter celebrations and it is a journey I can only really recommend to travellers with strong stomachs and even stronger behinds. The route is a fabulous one and crosses several high ranges of mountains. You travel practically the length of Greece and the experience costs around two pounds. (It is just your bad luck if you happen to be sitting next to a passenger inclined to bus sickness.) By the end of the journey you feel as if you had shared a deeply emotional and draining experience and know all your fellows intimately. You have joined in the rows about when and where to stop for lunch and partaken of all the sweetmeats and vegetarian delicacies that the Wise Virgins have packed in their dolly-bags, it being fast-time.

Everyone was v. kind to me because (a) I was a foreigner and (b) I looked so frail. By five o'clock in the afternoon we had dropped down into Igoumenitsa, a small seaside town from which there is a fairly frequent ferry-boat service to Corfu. Unfortunately, as the bus came to a grinding halt at the jetty we caught sight of the most recent sailing disappearing round the harbour entrance and no amount of screaming, abuse, or offers of gold would bring her back.

The bus clients, after hasty consultation, decided to take a caïque which was standing by—I imagine for just such an occurrence. Now that I know the idiosyncrasies of the Greeks and the adoration of nepotism which runs through the race, I suspect that the bus driver was a cousin of the caïque driver and had timed his arrival to a split second. I didn't give a hoot myself and it was all far more romantic on the small boat. Free coffee (solid grains as it turned out, only damp ones) was passed through the bridge window. It was indeed an 'aurea taxidi' (beautiful journey) and was accompanied by a great deal of community singing, not 'Roll out the Barrel' type stuff but sad quiet melodious numeros which went well with the ceiling of stars, which in those parts is so studded that it is sometimes v. difficult to find a bit of black, if you know what I mean.

We reached Corfu after about two and a half hours and the air was suddenly chill. As we approached the port there was sound of music and singing from the shore, and a huge illuminated cross, on top of the Old Port, contributed to the fairy-like atmosphere that I was about to take so indelibly to my heart. Though the approach was like a huge Cinemascope True Life Adventure (with no commentary, thank heaven), ashore it was like a Petrushka-type ballet. I think it is the grace of the Greeks which strikes one so enormously. No native of other races, it seems to me, can place the hand on the hip or the basket on the head with such beauty, and the lounging position, which can be so disastrously unattractive when practised by most Anglo-Saxons, can in Greece be a thing of great delicacy and dignity. I don't think I've ever encountered such natural gaiety and colour as that evening in Corfu. Many people were dressed in the national costume and the stores were stuffed with brightly-coloured goods. Thousands of Easter rabbits, hens, eggs and beautifully arranged bags and boxes of white sweets were on show, and though you will say 'So what? It's exactly the same in England' you would immediately see the difference taste-wise.

Everyone was carrying heavy parcels. Except me. I was carrying a typewriter and an exceptionally heavy suitcase. I thought it expedient to postpone my search for Mr Finney's villa till the following morning. After all I'd told him I'd clock in on Great Friday and now it was still Great Thursday (just). I slept in a strange little hotel called the Akropolis near the Old Port where we had docked. I had been solicited by the proprietor as I stepped off the caïque and, having been warned by my bus friends of the shortage of accommodation in the capital around this time of year, I said snap and was shortly in a ground-floor room containing five mattresses piled up on each other, and about a thousand

6

coat-hangers. It was then that I discovered that I was their first
guest ever: the proprietor had rumbled the fact that all accommodation in Corfu was filled to saturation point and had decided
to throw open what doors he had (attached to rooms, that is). I
couldn't close mine as the keys didn't seem to have arrived.

The Old Port was extremely noisy throughout the night and
the coat-hangers and I had a restless time of it. I was therefore up
early and found a bus reputedly going near Sotiriotissa, where
Albert's villa was. Owing to the word 'villa' being totally un-
Greek and ditto the name 'Carrer', it wasn't an easy job for a non-
Greek-speaking English gent to locate it and I eventually found it
by process of elimination or knocking off all the other largish
houses in the neighbourhood. I gathered it was absolutely exactly
where the bus had set me down in the first place, which was
somehow the last place in the world where I had expected to
find it.

I climbed up a long steep drive, with no name natch on the
gate, and found a large country house, with a superb view from
the windows of the sea, the Greek mainland and even Albania.
The house, as I know to my cost, couldn't be seen from the road
but I was glad of this, because while I was living there I used to
lean out of the window and pinch the oranges and lemons which
grew in great profusion in the garden. The fantastic colour of the
flowers and the lush foliage were my first sight of the tropical
splendour which spreads through the Ionian islands and makes
them so totally different from other parts of Greece. In order not
to persuade you to up sticks and leave immediately to take up
habitat permanently in the area, I must warn you that the winters
and springs can be wildly wet and cold and it is these that produce
all the super greenery. Weather up to the beginning of July can
be dodgy in the extreme and it is not until this month that King
Sol doth permanently doff his hat or whatever the nauseating
expression is.

It was, as a matter of fact, extremely cloudy when I rang the bell
at the Villa Carrer and the door was answered by Dmitri Calabas.
He turned out to be the Crichton of the joint—chauffeur, butler,

7

gardener and general factotum, who managed to make Albert and me feel remarkably silly when he served dinner in a white coat and we sat at opposite ends of the table looking like a couple of tramps who had wandered in by mistake. However, to relax the tension, it only needed Katina Foronachi, the pretty maid, to come backwards through the door carrying a tray and trying in vain not to giggle. Dmitri would speak sharply to her, which only made her laugh more. To complete the staff there was a cook called Marika Reggi and her moussaka had to be tasted to be disbelieved. Beautiful!

Albert had won them round with his infectious humour in next to no time and we were all great friends. We used to go out into the country together and the moment they left the house every inhibition vanished and they radiated spontaneous gaiety. They had been quite a long time in the service of Mr Carrer, who had retired to Corfu after surviving the big earthquake in Zante some decades earlier.

Anyhow Dmitri informed me that Kyrios (Mr) Albert was in the town looking for me so I waited around until he came back.

The next thirty-six hours were mostly spent in the capital being introduced to all Albert's Greek friends and watching the innumerable processions and rituals, which were enthralling to me. There was, for instance, the pot-throwing carry-on which takes place on Great Saturday at noon. It is then that suddenly all the top windows of the houses are opened and bits of pottery and jugs are emptied on the streets below, and heaven help you if you are standing in direct line of fire. There are also pilgrimages from church to church, and dozens of local bands, soldiers, sailors, scouts and guides, who march around, stopping to talk to friends who also happen to be onlookers. The whole thing culminates at midnight on Great Saturday, when the Square is filled with people and the Bishop ascends the steps of the bandstand and announces that Christ is Risen. On the receipt of this news, the crowd of thousands go movingly berserk. Everyone lights a candle and embraces his neighbour, songs and hymns are sung and millions of fireworks are let off. The whole experience is unforgettable and yet I don't want to see it again as it can never surpass the magic that sent my senses reeling the first time. It all seemed such a marvellously free release of love and happiness.

Most Greeks then go off and stuff themselves silly after their fast, though the wise ones save up for Easter Day when even the poorest family has a whole lamb to itself. This is the Meal of the Year and I'm not absolutely certain that it wasn't the Meal of the Century as far as I was concerned. I learned from Albert that we were having Easter lunch out.

'Where?' I asked.

'At Nikos the Fisherman's. Well, he's not really a fisherman but he's super.' The young actor and bon viveur had apparently gone on a series of trips with Nikos and on one occasion had caught a fish—oh that long and don't think any of us have ever heard the end of it. Anyhow he had been invited to the home of the Kaloudises (for that was Nikos's surname) for the tuck-in and oh yes he could bring his large friend with the healthy appetite.

We drove along to the little village of Ypsos about five miles north of the Villa Carrer towards the north of Corfu, which is so perilously near Albania. We got there about twelve-thirty and, by the side of the road where we stopped, two very large lambs were being roasted on spits. The aroma was breathtaking as they were being basted with some of the local herbs, and Ionian oil, which is just about the best in the world.

Albie introduced me to Nikos who was rushing back and forth from his house with tables and chairs. He refused to let us help him and I am bound to say that my first impression of him was that he was the healthiest man I'd ever seen. He is short and unbelievably brown, with the whitest teeth and the bluest eyes of anyone I know. He tells me that he has never brushed his teeth in his life but has just used salt water or salt and water, which goes to prove something or other. He has a ravishing smile, a balding head of hair and about as eccentric a command of the English language as you could hope for.

9

'Very very excuse me please' is still his way of apologizing and he has great difficulty with the sexes. All children are 'boys' and the Queen of Greece's pregnancy was conveyed to me quite simply by the phrase, 'Mrs King. Big stomach.' And yet his letters read like poems, particularly when one is thousands of miles away. Writing on lined midget pieces of paper, in some way he manages to enclose sun, sea and above all love. Some of the missives are terribly short:

'Dear Dear Friend Mr Peter. Your house very well. Nikki and boys send love. Never never forget. Your friend Nikos.'

Nikki Kaloudis is a handsome, dark but rather unhellenic young woman with a warm personality and a spirit of her own. Unlike some Greek wives she is brought into the foreground and she has a wonderful knack of making one feel at home. With no fuss at all she manages to produce super meals at a moment's notice and it is she who replies 'It is I who thank you' when I stammer out my few words of gratitude and appreciation.

Actually saying 'thank you' (epharisto) in Greek has presented no difficulties to me since a kind friend suggested that I should think of an American millionaire called F. Harry Stowe. So, with 'etsi-ketsi' (dodgy) and 'Po-Po-Po-Po' (Fancy! or, Oh goodness me!) I was able to make do, as all the dear Greeks require of one is that one should make an attempt to speak a word or two of their language so that they can fall about laughing.

Anyhow on this beautiful beautiful Easter Sunday language presented no difficulties and by the time we had had a couple of glasses of Nikos's home-made wine we were as happy as grigs. Everything on the table was from Nikos's smallholding. Home-made bread, cheese and wildly coloured salads and huge bowls of fruit littered the table; and even the poor lambs which were about to form the main course had till a few days before been gambolling in the Kaloudis pastures. There were several stacks of hard-boiled eggs painted red, which formed the basis for an age-old game played by the children—really exactly like conkers, only with eggs as weapons instead of chestnuts.

The Kaloudis children were already bashing at each other's

eggs, and a charming sight they were. Speroula, the younger, is remarkably pretty and blonde, an unusual hue in these parts. She has bags of personality and is a born mimic. In a short time she was sending Mr Finney and me up sky-high, copying our speech, behaviour and, I'm sorry to say, our table manners. Currently she has a romantic attachment for me, sealed by an engagement ring and, though I am dropped like a red-hot poker the moment Albert turns up, she remains fairly faithful apart from that. She is perhaps the Achilles heel of her otherwise seemingly perfect parents, and her excesses are smiled on. These include a marked penchant for consuming wine ('Chin Chin' and 'I'm happy to make your acquaintance' are her favourite expressions), a desire to be the centre of attraction all the time and an ability to get her own way consistently. These last two are achieved with the minimum of difficulty. It's not that she's precocious. Particularly. It's just that she's very feminine, very pretty and jolly sexy. And she knows it. She's every bit of eight years of age.

Her brother Yorgos suffers by comparison and is at his best when he's miles away from her and competition, and preferably acting as an efficient first mate to his father on the *Athena*, Nikos's boat which he uses for taking tourists, skin-divers or fishermen round the islands. He is ten years old (Yorgos I mean), blond, has a fair knowledge of English and can go to sleep standing up. Speroula on the other hand could go on drinking you under the table until well after midnight, I fancy.

At Easter lunch there were other members of the family. Nikki's mother, in the traditional black velvet and coiffed head-dress and bringing a bottle of Greek champagne to celebrate the occasion; her husband, neat and quiet; and a spit-turning brother and cousin completed the family gathering, and we were soon sitting down with all our trotters in the trough. Speaking for myself, I cannot remember ever eating so much at one sitting. Disgusting! Because that IS saying something.

After the feast, seeing that Mr Finney and I were in a state of near collapse, Nikos led us to an olive grove at the back of the house and laid us down on blankets and pillows. We were awakened by a small orchestra (average age seventy-five) playing 'Never On Sunday' over us, which was Nikos's idea of an alarm call.

Since my first Greek Easter I have spent two more with the Kaloudises and they have both been magical too. I took friends both times, people the family had never met, and they were as moved as I by the love and kindness radiating from Nikos and Nikki. There is a Greek word 'philoxenia', which translated literally means 'friend of strangers' (I may be wrong but I don't think this meaningful word appears in other languages) which seems to cover the extraordinary hospitality one receives from complete strangers in Greece. One cynical Athenian did say to me once: 'Oh yes, we LOVE strangers but HATE each other', which, I fear, remembering past history of civil and uncivil wars, has a smattering of truth in it. But I know for certain that, if I or any friend of mine were in any difficulty in Greece, Nikos would drop whatever he was doing and come rushing to the rescue.

These were early days and Albert knew Nikos far better than I, and their friendship was super to behold. There was no question of Nikos (or indeed any Corfiote) knowing anything about Mr Finney's meteoric career as none of his films had reached the capital. Incidentally when years later *Saturday Night and Sunday Morning* was shown in Corfu I took Nikos, who was, I fear, as disappointed as the rest of the inhabs. They simply didn't want to believe that there were such things as lathes and factories in England which they had previously imagined as being a land of large picture hats and Life Guards. I think Nikos quite liked Albie's disgraceful sexual behaviour in the film but in about five years' time when *Tom Jones* reaches them perhaps the balance will be adjusted, when they see the lords and ladies 'at it'!

On Easter Monday Albert suggested we might go on a boating trip with Nikos and was there anywhere I particularly wanted to visit?

'Yes. Paxos,' I said without a moment's hesitation.

I hadn't the foggiest idea where Paxos was but I remembered the name cropping up some thirty years previously when some friends of mine called Wilkinson had left England to live in Corfu. Later, when settled there, they had suggested to a family called Durrell that they might like it there too and we all know what that led to literary-wise, as I'm afraid our transatlantic cousins might say. Anyhow Mrs Wilkinson, who WAS the wife of my best friend who WAS Gerald Durrell's tutor and did indeed introduce him to the unique and fascinating Theodore Stephanides, asked me to stay out there *circa* 1932, an invitation which I was unable to accept. But correspondence between her husband George and me was fairly constant and what with the occasional jokey p.c. from L. Durrell, whom I'd also known in England, I formed a pretty good picture of Life Out There.

Now, though everyone in the preceding paragraph has pressed on a bit and married other persons, I am still in touch with most of the parties concerned and Mrs Wilkinson, who is now Mrs Macdonald, said to me, on hearing that I was visiting Corfu: 'By the way you might pop over to Paxos and see how my godson is getting on.'

'But of course,' I replied. 'What's the name of your godson?'

'Gordon. I don't think there are many people on Paxos with that name.' I thought she was probably right. She added that she hadn't seen him for thirty years and he might have grown a bit. She really wasn't a great deal of help.

So that was why I asked Albert if we could go to Paxos and said that I had heard from Mrs Macdonald-as-is that it was a Nice Place. He said I was name-dropping AND place-dropping and he'd ask Nikos the Fisherman what he thought of the idea. Nikos said it was a v. good idea—'Lovely place lovely peoples' is how he put it—and we were off. On the morning of our departure we went down to the little jetty in front of the villa and there was the *Athena*, Nikos's trim little caïque, bedecked with spring flowers. Katina and Marika had put them up and down the mast and along the guard rails and you have no idea how enchanting she looked. Down in the hold were picnic baskets galore, casks of wine and great stone jars of water, and anyone would have thought we were off on an odyssey.

The weather was perfect and we travelled the length of Corfu in calm seas, stopping every now and then for a bit of fishing. In about five hours we arrived at the northern tip of Paxos having crossed the ten-mile channel between the islands. At first sight the smaller island looked uninhabited and all one could see for the eight miles of its length was olive-trees. Sailing within a few hundred yards of the coast, we were able to catch glimpses of the caves nearly a mile deep, that housed resistance Greeks during the war. At the southern tip of the island we saw Antipaxos about a mile away and decided to explore that. Nikos said we could circle it in very little time and return to Paxos—to Gaios, the capital—for the night. In fact we found a little cove in Antipaxos about which we were so potty that we decided to spend the night there. We swam and swam and Albie missed a tiny octopus at practically point-blank range with his underwater gun. Not best pleased he wasn't and we would have enjoyed it for dinner over the little fire we rigged up on the beach. After dinner we walked a bit but there were few signs of habitation. About forty people live on Antipaxos, fishermen mostly, though the seasonal cultivation of vines for Antipaxos wine is profitable. A great deal of it is shipped over to the mother island. But Antipaxos is a rarely visited place, though it possesses one ravishing sandy beach, which canny Corfiotes know about and hie to. Otherwise it is just a sea of olive-trees.

We were wakened just before dawn by the hideous whistling of a great wind and the sound of lashing rain. We poked our heads out of the hold and caught sight of Nikos casting off from the anchorage. We threw on some clothes and made a pretence of looking shipshape, seamanlike and like crew members. I kept on thinking of old nautical phrases I'd learned during the war like 'Heave away handsomely' and 'Avast', which wasn't franchement much help to anyone, but luckily our skipper seemed in full command of the situation and assured us that there was no cause for alarm. Actually we couldn't have taken to the boats even if he'd ordered it as there weren't any, except the one we were in at the time. 'Little wind. Dead soon,' said Nikos, as we left our cove a bit bumpily. But there was no protection there from this particular wind and Nikos announced that we were going to look for alternative shelter. Five minutes later we were coming alongside a small jetty a little to the south of where we had been. It was now almost light and the sky looked pretty terrifying. Racing pitch-black clouds were hurtling across and there was a chill air of impending doom. After five years seafaring I had lost any love I had had for the open sea. I like it tight closed myself.

As we were tying up, some fishermen emerged from a hut nearby. All their boats, I noticed, were drawn up on a rocky beach a few yards away and there wasn't a sausage except us afloat. There was a great deal of shaking of heads as they chatted to Nikos and it was plain that optimism wasn't exactly rampant. However it was equally clear that our gallant captain was not to be discouraged, and though we didn't like to ask him to issue a series of bulletins it was obvious that he was working out a Plan of Campaign.

Suddenly he announced to all and sundry, 'Go to Paxos now.' He instructed an Antipaxiot to cast us off and we retreated into the steaming sea, to the accompaniment of a good deal of muttering and crossing themselves by the onlookers. It didn't take an old salt like me long to realize that we were in for a Buffeting and already the small channel between the islands, which we had covered in a flash twelve hours ago, looked interminable. There was a colossal sea running and I did a bit of figurative crossing myself. I only remembered one occasion during the war when I had been terrified to this extent. (See *To Sea In a Sieve* by the same author. Out of print. So sucks!)

I took up my position amidships, half-hidden and protected by the hatch down to the hold. I watched Albert and Nikos standing in the stern at the tiller, their faces filled with a strange exaltation, and taking every scenic-railway type dip with roars of laughter.

Of progress there was little and I couldn't believe that we would end up anywhere except at the bottom of the Ionian Sea. The sea came sloshing over the bows and nearly every wave knocked me silly, so that I kept ducking like an Aunt Sally (does she duck or doesn't she duck?) to avoid the onslaught. Finally I thought it expedient to return to the hold and lie prone, resigning myself to certain death calmly and as befitted a Lieut.-Commander R.N.V.R. (retired). The Heroes, soaked to the skin and greeting every torrent like a long-lost brother, neither approved nor condemned my action and just waved happily as if they were standing on the balcony of Buckingham Palace.

I must have been down in the hold for at least an hour before I came out of my coma sufficiently to realize that the ship had stopped lurching. Could we perhaps have been transplanted to some Astral Plane? I rose groggily to my feet and emerged cautiously but bravely. I saw that we were close inland and rapidly approaching a harbour entrance with a very narrow opening. We had made Gaios, which is in a unique position to give shelter from the elements because it has not one but two islets bang in front of it so that the inner channel is as protected as any harbour in the world. It can also be entered from either side.

Indeed as we passed the harbour lights we found ourselves in the proverbial millpond. I recovered rapidly but Nikos and Albie looked a tidge disappointed that it was all plain sailing now. The *Athena* was clearly delighted and glided happily to her berth at the far end of the town, where willing hands issued from side streets to tie her up.

Well, I had regained my spirits but not my balance, and in a frenzy to touch down on dry land again I lost all sense of propriety and behaved like a really irresponsible teenager, jumping off the ship with such abandon that I injured my heel agonizingly. Poor old Alb had the tough end of this one as for the next few days I was to hobble round the town, leaning not unheavily on his shoulder.

But even with this mishap it didn't take me long to realize that

16

the people of Paxos were pretty special. Nikos seemed to know most of the local inhabitants and during the two days and nights we spent in Gaios we were wined and dined extensively and, because we had decided to sleep on board, blankets and pillows arrived in embarrassing quantities. The weather improved and we got away from Paxos just in time to greet Tony Richardson and Vanessa Redgrave who were spending a brief honeymoon on Corfu. We were swimming in the sea by the Kaiser's Bridge and suddenly glimpsed them and we all went and had a super tuck-in at the Avra restaurant, which overlooks Mouse Island and the beautiful Kanoni Point. When we finally got back to the villa the staff gave us an hysterical welcome, having given us up for lost.

The Richardsons had to leave almost immediately and our time in Corfu was drawing to a close. We had apparently one other festivity to attend, details of which seemed difficult to obtain. 'Dancing Sunday at Barbardy. Marvellooose,' Nikos kept saying but it was gibberish to us. However we did understand we had to be on the small jetty in front of the Costas Hotel at Ypsos at a certain time and then all would be clear. We were going dancing in a boat, which seemed a bit etsi-ketsi to me. We went with the entire staff of the Villa Carrer, all tarted up to the nines, and when we arrived in Ypsos there was a very gay scene indeed. A wedding was in full swing, or rather a wedding lunch, and some pretty fancy dancing was going on to the accompaniment of the elderly orchestra who had serenaded us on Easter Sunday.

Albert and the girls started to dance and a boat (not Nikos's) drew into the jetty and embarked the long queue of waiting customers. All of them, we noticed, were wearing their Sunday best and every girl had high heels on, which we couldn't imagine would be ideal for open-air dancing. But it was Sunday, as yet a pretty special day in these parts, and young men dressed in dark suits with ties melded with the girls in their best summer frocks. In the little villages particularly you find a great difference from other days in the week. Ikons have lights placed in front of them

17

in cafés, houses and shrines; buses play religious services on their radios; and the richer and more sophisticated inhabitants listen to ditto on their transistor radios, which they carry round attached to their lug-holes.

This afternoon there was a certain amount of not entirely suppressed gaiety in the air and when Nikos's beaming face appeared at the helm of the *Athena* he took a pretty boisterous crowd aboard. The ship was once again decorated with flowers, and not for the first time in Corfu did Albie and I regret having dressed 'down' and not 'up' for the occasion. People kept on arriving, brought by lorry, motor cycle, mule or feet. We were packed like sardines into the boat and it took us three-quarters of an hour to reach our destination. Nikos dropped his anchor over the stern and the *Athena* slid up a rocky beach. Planks were placed over her bows and the customers were helped ashore.

The sight that met our eyes was about the prettiest I remember in all my puff. Beneath the mountains was a large stretch of greensward, filled with masses of people from every village for miles. There was one house, which was empty, and the sides of the meadow were flanked by tables and chairs. Spread all round were cakes, sweets, wine and toys. There were two three-piece orchestras playing alternately and the 'dancing' had already started.

You, gentle reader, will be thinking, 'What is he banging on about? It sounds just like a village fête to me.' And of course you are right and it's extremely difficult to explain why a Greek festa is so special. I would say the difference lies mainly in the total lack of self-consciousness at enjoyment and happiness. There is a spirit of love and humanity in the air which transcends ordinary gatherings and one is, as a stranger, drawn into this by a kind of magical force. I have never felt forlorn or lonely at any Greek get-together yet often at parties or even dinners with chums in London an ineffable feeling of not being part of it has flowed over me.

I think part of the breathtaking gaiety of a Greek festa is that everyone behaves as if none of the modern forms of entertainment exist and we are entirely dependent on each other to keep going. At Barbardy that afternoon I know I felt that this was what life was all about. Just Communication in its simplest form—people talking, dancing, and getting together for no particular reason, and expecting, giving and receiving nothing except friendliness and love.

Over the scene Nikos hovered, with a vast grin on his dear nut-brown face. It was he and the other caïque owner who had made the afternoon possible and the occasion summarized his philosophy: 'All good company. Little drinking. Little eating. Much loving. All friends together.' This is the recurring theme of his outlook on life; to him nothing in the world is as important as people being nice to each other. I simply will not call it 'togetherness' because that word always alarms me deeply. It reminds me of Brighton beach on August Bank Holiday or the Players' Club when the chairman asks us all if we are happy, a question which plunges me into deep gloom.

But with Nikos the wish for mankind is crystal-clear and beautiful. I think his philosophy is pretty well expressed in a poem called 'The Wish', which was written by a young American poet, Richard Caplin, before he was eighteen years of age. For some unknown reason his work remains unpublished on both sides of the Atlantic. He wrote:

> the wish i wish now
> is to marry the whole world and be
> the father and mother and brother and sister to
> the funnyugly fat and the skinthin and the
> pretty men girls and
> the very lovely forever, to be
> a family reunion in myself
> strong awake and full of milk and eggs
> i wish joy were green then i would be your
> grass, garden, trees-green, green, green,
> for a year of sundays and never go away . . .
> i wish i were green forever.

The lack of capitals is the poet's doing, not mine. It is just that the moment i read it i thought of nikos the fisherman.

The trouble with writing about Nikos is that I'll probably make him sound like a boring saint and that's the last thing he is. But he does seem to me fairly unique and there are so many qualities in his character that are rare enough singly. I have never known him to be unkind to anyone or to mistrust them at first meeting. I have seen him drunk, and in dreadful pain, yet nothing seems to ruffle his faith in life and human nature. He does get irritated by other people's lack of faith and I recall an excruciatingly funny occasion when I was trying to hitch-hike back from his house to Corfu one night. We stopped dozens of cars and everyone seemed perfectly willing to take Nikos anywhere but the moment they saw me lurking in the background they got windy. Finally I went and hid behind a tree. A car stopped and after a short confab with the driver Nikos beckoned me to approach. I saw the driver's face fall and he started arguing with Nikos in Greek. He did finally give me a lift but apparently was convinced, because of my very red face and apoplectic demeanour, that I was a dangerous drunk.

At Barbardy that afternoon there was none of that distrust. No one doubted that he would be taken back home, and as the sun started to sink behind the mountains the caïques embarked 'the whole company'. The wedding party was still in progress at Ypsos when we got back and some of the guests were trying to twist, an experiment which captured Albert's attention, and he was soon gyrating like a top. Katina was an apt pupil and they were applauded wildly.

We got back into the car eventually and Dmitri became quite suddenly the perfect butler and wished to know What We Wanted For Dinner. It all seemed a bit dotty to us and we said we didn't mind a damn what we had and would probably cook it ourselves so there! In that case, said Dmitri, could we all spare the time to come and see his old Mum. She'd never seen Albie or me and she'd like that. We'd like that too, we said. Back at the Villa

Carrer, we didn't seem able to muster a key between us so Katina took off her shoes, rolled up her skirt, and scaled up a huge olive-tree like a monkey and climbed in through one of the windows and let us in.

A few minutes later, after we'd put on Our Woollies (it can be nippy at night in April even in Greece), we followed Dmitri down a winding path at the back of the house in the moonlight. In ten minutes we came to a Hansel and Gretel witch-type house surrounded by olive-trees. Inside there was a tiny wizened old lady without a tooth in her head, who didn't seem remotely put out by the sudden cavalcade (for Katina and Marika had joined us) and gave us a ravishing smile of welcome. In fifteen minutes flat, aided by her son, she had trotted out her best crockery, glasses and linen and prepared a meal apparently out of the air. It had great variety and went a bit towards proving my theory that, for the Greeks, sitting down to a big meal among themselves is unknown: they just exist on bread, olive oil and fetta (Greek goat's cheese of strongish pong), but if a stranger or guest comes to their doors they give him, her or them everything but the kitchen stove.

Throughout the evening neighbours clocked in and soon we were singing away with a lot of lovely old toothless Greek ladies.

It was just the way to celebrate our last night in Corfu.

The next morning was as emotional a one as I can recall. I opened my window quite early to grab a last orange or four and saw the *Athena* waiting at the jetty, freshly decorated with flowers, and Nikos in his Sunday best though it was Monday. When we were ready to leave we had to face a send-off from the Villa Carrer. Mr Carrer told us that his staff would never get over us and our friendliness and Katina and Marika brought bunches of flowers and there was a lot of hugging and crying and we got on the boat as quickly as poss. Dmitri was to join us at the airport with the luggage, and on the short voyage to the Old Port Nikos gave us fresh nuts, chickens and wine from his house, to say nothing of the precious olive oil. At the airport we were joined by the entire Kaloudis family, the children having never been so close to an aeroplane before. After a series of heartbreaking embraces we got aboard. My last sight of Corfu was Nikos crossing himself and I knew we were in safe hands.

2. Land in Paxos

Back in England it wasn't long before I was conscious of one thought coursing through my brain day and night: I must build a house in Paxos. I kept seeing in front of my eyes the little harbour, the olive trees, the cleanness and stillness of it all, the turquoise sea and above all the faces of the people. It became such an obsession with me that I found it creeping into all my shopping lists. 'Frozen salmon fishcakes—Energen Crispbread—Land in Paxos' was the sort of thing that bewildered anyone looking over my shoulder. As it never got crossed off I had it continually in front of me both in dreams and real life.

By a freak of chance two very good friends of mine, Tony Oliver and Peter Sutton, were planning a holiday and asked me my views on Corfu. I steered them straight into going there, at first with no ulterior motive, but just before they went I couldn't resist asking them if they'd mind popping over to Paxos to make a few inquiries into the Real Estate Market there. They came back with a great many photographs of Lakka, a small village on the island, and an alarming story of how the Americans were drilling for oil outside Gaios. This situation had not unnaturally thrown the entire population into a frenzy of anticipation and hope. The price of land had rocketed and my chums were not hopeful about my prospects. I am bound to say that I was completely taken aback. Quite apart from my own disappointment it was inconceivable that Paxos should become a huge commercial venture, dominated by Edward G. Robinson type characters, and 'gushers', my dear, absolutely EVERY-WHERE!

I wrote to Nikos the Fisherman explaining the latest development and asked him if he'd be so kind as to keep an eye on the situation. I had already decided to go out to Corfu again in the spring and you can imagine with what relief and delight I received a letter from Nikos saying, 'Americanos go away. No oil. Come quick. Come Pasqua. All good company. Much drinking. Much eating. Never Forget. Your friend Nikos.' So I came Pasqua and there was much eating and much drinking. I also took part in the Easter procession, led by the hand by little Speroula, and we went from church to church in pilgrimage. There were constant stops along the roadside for prayers and blessings and heaven didn't exactly help the motor cars and cycles which tried to pass during these periods. Scenes of vituperation and piety were finely mingled and the noise was considerable. Any foreigner must have been bewildered but fascinated, and pictorially it was a moving sight, with groups of old ladies falling on their knees and crossing themselves by the wayside and waiters leaving tables at cafés or hotels to do likewise.

A few days later we set off in the *Athena* for Paxos. This time we made straight for the capital. I had banged on so long in letters and chat about exactly what I wanted that Nikos knew my requirements by heart and used to chant them to me in a sort of litany. 'Very very quiet place. No peoples. Much writing. No telephones. Much writing. Not much money.' He would then add, to show our indomitable spirits, 'Looking. No Good. Never mind. Always more looking.' And that's how it happened. We were always looking. It didn't take long for the news to circulate round the good but astute people of Gaios that I was in the market for land and after the obvious disappointment of the oil failure there was, Nikos reported, a sharp drop in price levels. I went on a tour of the town, jotting down in my block (Greek for 'block') measurements, details, costs and a lot of hieroglyphics which I didn't understand myself but thought might impress the crowd who accompanied us on our meanderings.

We saw many beautifully situated plots of land but somehow they were all too obviously enclosed in territory that I could see being overrun by tourist development in the next few years. And, though I realize now I should have bought every bit of acreage or hectarage I could, it really isn't my cup of tea. The buying and selling lark, I mean, whether it's earth or Wedgwood teapots. Too lazy that's what I am. Anyhow, as at that time the new direct jet service from London to Corfu was about to start operating, the extra sea-mileage was not going to prevent an eventual run on Paxos. Perhaps, I mused, I would have to retreat to Antipaxos. No, I could still see those gloomy fishermen on the wooden jetty. AntiP. would be just a bit too far 'away from it all'. And yet that spring morning in Gaios there seemed little tangible evidence that here was an incipient St Tropez. True, there was the beginning of a coast road which, like all similar Greek enterprises, ended quite suddenly in a practically impracticable cart track, owing to the money running out. There were also several partially completed houses which I was offered at anything but cut rates. The Greeks are nothing if not optimistic and were asking astronomical prices for brick shells, already providing housing for shrubs, cats, goats and the contents of dustbins.

We spent the night in the port and I paid the equivalent of two shillings and sixpence for a bed in a spotless house near the sea, and the old dear who ran it gave me a lot of home-made cakes to take on my way. After seeing a few more possible sites Nikos suggested that we should start back but call in at Lakka on the way. This was the village to the north of the island which Tony Oliver had cased the previous year. We set sail, passing on our route Loggos, the third harbour of Paxos, which was pretty as a picture but just too remote for me. Though the incoming and outgoing ferry-boats pay a daily visit it is two miles from the bus stop and has very few shops. But all the houses are yellow and pink with green shutters and from the sea it looks ravishing. The water by the tiny jetty is as clear as spring water and you can see the bottom at forty feet.

So many of these villages look like rather modern toy-towns, that you see made out of square wood in shops for avant-garde children. But somehow the designers can never quite catch the soft whitewash colouring that the Greeks achieve so effortlessly. Nikos, for instance, painted my kitchen in some left-over mixture which is quite breathtakingly pretty. A sort of Botticelli blue against which the yellow crockery doesn't look half bad. But the worrying thing about the Greeks is how, in spite of their seemingly faultless taste in colour, they have taken so eagerly to the worst plastic and neon excesses. And the modern furniture shops seem to me to resemble the Chamber of Horrors at Madame Tussaud's as usually the owners are splayed about over the wares. Anyhow as yet the older houses in Paxos are happily free from all this junk and are simply but beautifully furnished with handmade carpets and antique heavy wooden wardrobes and commodes, if that's the word.

Anyhow here we are pressing on to Lakka or we were a page ago before I started carrying on about something I know nothing about. The harbour of Lakka is situated between two rocky headlands, on the top of one of which is a ruined church and on the top of the other—well that's another story. No! I'm a liar. It's this story. But you must wait a sec. It was eleven o'clock before we tied up alongside the jetty and the daily ferry-boat had just left. There were two oil-lamp lamp-posts to greet us which were joined later by a handful of residents, most of whom Nikos seemed to know intimately. We adjourned (all of us) to what I discovered later to be the Hub of the Town. This was Spiro Theophrastus Petrou's Café, a largish, completely square building, which serves as post office, telephone exchange, cinema, sweet shop, and committee rooms. Official notices are posted there, newspapers seem to find their way there even if a few days late, and business conclaves are held at and around those tables not already occupied by persons playing backgammon or cards.

Good news travels fast in small villages and strangers seem to have the same effect on the inhabs as lamps have on moths. In a very short time Spiro's Café was thronged with prospective landlords and amateur estate agents. Ten minutes later I found myself facing the olive groves that T. Oliver had photographed. I showed the snaps to my small band of followers who were overcome with wonder and excitement at this miracle of timing and obviously couldn't understand how I had got hold of them.

The plot of land which was apparently being offered me during all this to-do was picturesque, to put it mildly, being situated in the middle of a terrace of perfectly matched stones which must have been there for over five hundred years. It was however a tidge too near a building which served as the local abattoir, judging from the skins hanging up outside and the sinister red stains on the floor. I entered a series of hieroglyphics feverishly in my block but shook my head at Nikos who said, 'Never mind. Always looking.'

A strangely tall gent with white hair and some curious pink pigmentation on his forehead, culminating in a not absolutely bewitching carbuncle, detached himself from the group and said a few words to Nikos, and we started trekking past the school-house and up a steep hill. We saw a couple of houses on the way, one old and one modern, but when we reached the crest of the hillside via a stony path, there was no sign of habitation.

We found ourselves on a small plateau overlooking the Ionian Sea from which one could see Corfu and a long stretch of the Greek mainland. In the far distance there was the outline of Pantocrator, the highest peak in Corfu, and within a very large stone's throw of Albania. Just below our feet was a carpet of broom and below that a stretch of sea, the colour of which I find indescribable. Turquoise is the nearest to it but as that word is of Turkish origin I had better not use it to describe Greek water. Right opposite the cliff on which we were poised was the ruined church I have already referred to, and below it, through a gap in the cliff face, one could see a formation of rocks in the sea, purporting to be the petrified remains of Ulysses' ship.

It was just about as perfect a spot as one could imagine. The scent of spring flowers had gone whizzing up my nostrils and made me a little light-headed. I looked at Nikos and said, 'This is the Place', a pronunciamento I gather the head of the Mormons made when he and his followers arrived at the spot which was eventually to become Salt Lake City. If he'd persevered and pressed on he would undoubtedly have reached California, which would have yielded him more worldly wealth, I imagine, than Utah. Still I think he was quite content with his original choice, and I can say after three halcyon years that goes for me too.

But, over-excited though I was, I was determined to try to play it cool as I could see Kyrios Ypsilos (Mr Tall) watching me like a lynx ('lynx' in Greek).

I said to Nikos in English: 'It is very far from the village and where is the water?'

This was a master-stroke and Mr Tall looked v. embarrassed when Nikos said 'Poo einai nero;' (Where is water?)

A few minutes later I found myself the owner of a small plot of Greek soil for the equivalent of forty pounds. Though Nikos opined that it was 'polla lepta' (many pennies) it seemed to me a miraculous buy. We adjourned to the house of Mr Ypsilos (for that is what I shall call him from now on) where a slightly alarmed Mrs Ypsilos served us tiny cups of turcico, as the Greeks still name their coffee in spite of the Unpleasantness. On the way upstairs I had unwisely admired a white bird hanging on the wall. On the way downstairs I was presented by Mr Ypsilos with a kiss on both cheeks and the bird, which turned out to be a freshly shot seagull, by mistake. Shot by mistake I mean. It upset me so much on the voyage home in the *Athena* that I had to bury it at sea, to stop its poor feathers fluttering in the wind, Pavlova fashion.

Before we set sail, Mr Ypsilos made arrangements with Nikos to come over to Corfu to sign the documents transferring the piece of land to him, Nikos, for no foreigner can buy land or build houses in this part of the world. It is chiefly in areas near a frontier (in this case the Albanian one) that this impasse arises; to overcome it is a laborious and sometimes heartbreaking task. You have first to find a Greek sponsor you can trust implicitly and arrange with him that he either mortgages the land to you, gives it to you after a certain period, or leaves it to you in his will. The Greek government has apparently no jurisdiction over gifts though I may have got it wrong as usual. But I have put this all in as a cautionary word for those suddenly seized with a desire to hootle off and try to buy up large sections of Hellas.

But having Nikos as my friend meant that I was sitting comparatively pretty. When I got back to Corfu and told various people about my plans they were at first inclined to be sceptical, but I had only to mention the name of Nikos Kaloudis for their faces to light up immediately. 'Ah. Nikos Kaloudis. Well, that's different.' He is immensely respected the length and breadth of Corfu and I love watching him acknowledge the continual greetings which meet us when we are walking through the town.

Anyhow he handled the whole thing quite beautifully and didn't ask ghastly questions all the time. When it came to the stage of deciding what sort of house I wanted, I had only to point out my preference when we were on a walk. 'Nikos, dear friend, windows like that, please. Door like that. Colour the same' and so on. He wrote it all down in his block and I don't think I doubted for a single second that when I arrived the following year I should find the identical house of which I had dreamed. I left him a little money and when I went to America with *Luther* that autumn I was able to send regular dollops.

By the early spring my thoughts were constantly centred on that small plateau in the Ionian island of Paxos. My imagination was fanned by regular short notes from Nikos, all of which followed roughly the same pattern:

'Dear dear friend Mr peter. I am in Lakka for your work. Here is badwether, all rens, snows, your house is well, room well. I took your lovely books for boys. I thank you very very very very very very very very very much, my children thank you for thinks. And for your good company. Soon much drinking, Nikki to love you and boys. Never forget. Much love. Your friend Nikos.'

I got out to Corfu on 1 April 1964 and the weather was pretty ghastly. After several Aprils and Mays out here I have come to the regrettable conclusion that the warm Mediterranean spring sun is a myth and that until at least the middle of June one cannot 'count on the weather', as my mother would have said. In the spring it is just as likely to be rainy and cold as it is in uptown Kensington. And much colder INDOORS, owing to the lack of heating in all but the most modern houses and hotels. So, what with the inclemency of the weather and all, it was deemed unwise to take Nikos's *Athena* to Paxos, and, seeing my obvious impatience, we went at earliest opportunity by ferry-boat. It was the *Aspasia* on this occasion and as service between the islands had been suspended for several days she was crammed with human and animal passengers. Nikos sat in a corner reading *To Bema*, the leftish Athenian newspaper to which he is addicted. He sat as he always does in that curious position in which he seems to become part of the vessel's fittings. I can't explain it any other way, but I know that when he's at the tiller of his own boat he suddenly looks as if he'd never been anywhere else. If I am away from him for a long time I try to bring him before my eyes and it is always in this image that he materializes.

On the way to Paxos we stopped at Cavos at the south of Corfu where we took a good many sheep aboard, tied to each other by the feet and lying meekly bleating on the deck, realizing only too well that Easter was at hand and that they weren't long for this world anyhow. Anyhow we all had a roughish tossing through the channel and fifty per cent of the passengers were very sick indeed. Nikos went quietly on reading *To Bema*. Suddenly he put it down, arose, beckoned to me and pointed at the land ahead.

'Mr Peter,' he announced, 'To Spiti Sou' (Your House). And I could just discern miles away a small white being. As we got nearer I saw two windows with green shutters and a green door.

Nikos watched my face and came and put an arm on my shoulder and I am bound to say my excitement was becoming almost unbearable. The nearer one got to it, the more one became conscious of the fact that To Spiti Mou (My House) was not just the first building but the only one visible from the sea. It has become a sort of legend in these parts and I am a very proud man. Complete strangers on the ferry-boat come up to me and tell me that it's My House and I see people look at it with admiration and, I hope, envy. It is in a unique position because, though it is invisible from any other building and from the village which is a few minutes walk away, I can watch from it all incoming sea traffic. Tourists, friends, enemies and rich yachts come under my microscopic (or telescopic) scrutiny and there is plenty of time to down shutters and take to the hills if one doesn't like the look of what the tide is bringing in.

But on this afternoon I was filled with love of humanity and I was greatly moved by the warm welcome the small crowd on the jetty gave me. They wished me great joy and happiness (Nikos translated for me) and we had a quick turcico at Spiro's Café. Nikos excused us as soon as he decently could. But not before the schoolmaster had told him that if I wanted any painting done I had only to say the word and he would send a selection of his pupils up. It turned out that it was a selection of his pupils who sent me up. But that's life, that's what that is!

We climbed the steep cliff and I am bound to admit that I was in such terrible condition that I began to think that I had made a tiny error in my choice of location and was in for a series of strokes before I actually reached it. But when we started down the drive ($1\frac{1}{2}$ft wide) I knew that I had not made a mistake.

Now you may think, like so many of my friends, that there is nothing more boring than people telling you about their dreams. Well, I think you are wrong and that there is, and it is telling you How Their Dreams Have Come True. So hang on to your hats, keep down the bile and give me, prithee, your indulgence.

For the whole of the previous year in buses, streets, dressing-rooms and certainly in the privacy of my own home I had been picturing what It would be Like, and there It was. You see, why I am going on so is because it's never happened to me before. Things exactly as you imagined them, I mean. Holidays, leaves,

reunions, books, films, love affairs, plays and parties. How rarely has the reality come anywhere near the expectation!

But with To Spiti Mou it was different. From close-to outside, it looked rather like a little squat toby jug, friendly and clean-cut. Inside it was as yet almost bare, apart from a wash-basin in the kitchen, complete with tap, and a flushing cistern in To Meros (the Loo), representing the only modern convenience of which I was not going to deprive myself.

There was just enough space in the one room to put two beds and later a huge wardrobe to store everything. 'Big box coming,' said Nikos reassuringly. To him every container is a box be it a bottle, a tin, a wine cask, an oil drum or even a box.

I just stood looking at the whitewashed walls and the scarcely dry brick-red floor.

'Is good?' asked Nikos the Fisherman.

'Is very good, dear Nikos,' I replied giving him a great bear hug. It was too early to assess the full measure of his achievement and therefore I was unable to express my gratitude adequately except emotionally. One had first to take into account the sheer physical labour of getting all the bricks, cement, etc. up the hill by mule(s) and having no water in the immediate vicinity, apart from the rain, which had been heavy that winter and delayed progress on the house. Nikos had built the whole thing himself with the help of a few Paxiots for just over two hundred quid and it was a miracle. It was also the same as his original estimate which is not, leave us face it, excessive for a Dream Come True. He had used considerable ingenuity and at the back of the little house, tilted at an angle, was a maroon-coloured oil drum which was to house the water brought daily from the village by Nikos's friend, Alekkos Apergis, who was to be my factotum and invaluable counsellor and to whom I was to be handed over. A small trim balding man, far more serious than Nikos, but a tower of strength with his two mules and if one ran out of gas, water, food or conversation at parties.

But there is no one quite like Nikos and his sensitivity is such that he knew exactly what was in my mind. He knew that I wanted to sleep in To Spiti Mou even if there were no beds, bedding or furniture and it was as cold as charity and far damper. So we trotted down to the little village and had a fairly peculiar meal in the only restaurant in Lakka, run by a dear little man called Spiro, as indeed are fifty per cent of the male population. The chef's own dish that evening was 'Entrail Soup', which wasn't nearly as repellent as it sounds. Later, when I discovered that both 'Stuffed Spleen' and 'Bread-Crummled Brain Balls' were considered high delicacies, nothing in the bill of fare surprised me. I do suspect however that 'Crummled' was meant to be 'crumbed'. I remember once in Spain ordering 'Hurried Eggs' which was the way they described this simple dish (Scrambled dittos).

Nikos disappeared during the meal and reappeared carrying a heap of bedding he'd borrowed from a friend and we took the path back to My House. I asked Nikos if he'd like to sleep there but he wisely declined, preferring the comparative comfort of his ship. He laid the bedding on the floor and tucked me in.

I said good night to him and pretended to be half asleep. A few minutes after he'd left me, shining his torch in front of him down The Drive, I was out on My Terrace, mixing with the fireflies and watching the way the beam from the lighthouse struck softly on me every time it gyrated. It would be very effective when one was entertaining of an evening, I thought to myself as I clambered down into my bed. I could pretend that I had laid it on myself. Oh, how marvellous it was all going to be! I felt immensely happy. 'Must get a table and chairs,' I muttered to myself before dropping off.

I cannot begin to pretend that my first night in To Spiti Mou was a success. I was far too excited to sleep, and far too cold, and the smell of new paint was fairly asphyxiating. I was down in the village at dawn looking for coffee. And found it. For Spiro's Café opens up nice and early to cater for customers leaving for the capital on the seven o'clock bus. Nikos was already there discussing my problems with the inhabitants.

Most of the furniture and fittings had to be brought from

Corfu and I now had an interminable shopping list in my mind so we caught the morning ferry-boat home, after Nikos had painted the floors of To Spiti Mou yet again. It was a peach of a day and we travelled in 'The Pullman', the ship that I was to get to know so well later. Mitsos, the skipper, was a close friend of Nikos's and we all had a jolly alfresco lunch of bread, olive oil and Greek cheese.

Safely back in Corfu there was masses to do. My first guest, a painter from Atlanta, Georgia, called Nelson Jennings, was due any minute and was very tall indeed. This fact involved going round measuring beds as they stood up against the walls outside shops. Most Greeks are short and I was to have the same trouble with sheets until Nikos's friend Mrs Vlachos came to the rescue. She helped me buy the linen by the yard and then took me to her private sempstress to complete the job. A remarkably kind lady who acted as interpreter between Nikos and me over money matters, which made us nervous. Money matters I mean. Mrs Vlachos had a knack of making everything crystal-clear. She always looked so cool too in white with a blue bandeau round her pretty head. When I first met her she was running a very reasonable little hotel called the San Rocco, where I stayed on and off.

Nelson arrived and we struck a patch of frightfully bad weather which rather spoiled things, as he, to say nothing of me, was dying to get to Paxos. But the ferry-boats were not running and we lived from day to day surrounded by the household goods and getting tetchier hourly. Finally one midday we were sitting having luncheon in Corfu with the illustrator of this book and his dear wife, Inez, when Nikos suddenly appeared at the table.

'*Aspasia* going Paxos in ten minutes. Come quick,' he announced. We were down at the Old Port in a flash, and aided by a taxi or two and Nikos's seemingly superhuman strength we were able to get ourselves and all our chattels aboard the ferry-boat just as she was beginning to hoot hysterically to gather in the latecomers. We distributed beds, mattresses, tables and chairs among the goats and passengers already assembled and in a few

35

minutes we were off. It was a rainy, blustery day and we spent most of the voyage in the open, as cabin conditions, to put it mildly, were not overwhelmingly fragrant.

Truth to tell everything went wrong on this very important day and for the first time in the history of the enterprise somehow I lost heart and My Dream was turning rapidly into My Nightmare. It was too rough to get into Lakka harbour and we pressed on to Loggos where we had an interminable wait. By the time we reached Gaios it was getting dark and we were damp, cold and dispirited and wished we were back in the San Rocco Hotel with all those jolly maids banging about.

Only Nikos was unperturbed and remained so even when we discovered that, as it was Sunday, the bus to Lakka was not running. The telephone exchange was equally out of commission and, after consulting some of the local inhabs in the town square, Nikos took us to a lodging-house where he persuaded us to have a lie-down. He then disappeared to some unknown destination, to reappear an hour later with the sensational news that the bus would be in Gaios directly. It wasn't till later that I realized what a feat it was to get the driver of 'Hoi Dio Adelphoi' ('The Two Brothers', as the bus is called and it is the only one on the isle) to leave his quiet Sunday at home and rescue two foreign persons from despair.

When we got down to the square again we found that Nikos had packed the back of the bus with our goods and we took to the road. I think we were the only passengers at that point though we were joined later by some customers in Magazia, which is a village lying inland to the centre of Paxos. In half an hour we were outside Spiro Café where most of the village seemed to be assembled—a late hour for them (tennish). I saw Mr Ypsilos zooming down towards us.

Nelson, whose first visit to Europe it was, was bewildered and cold and we were both dead on our feet. Nikos, ever sensitive, took matters in hand, quietly abstracted what we needed for the night from the luggage and we were off up the hill. He settled us in and went back to the village to sleep in Spiro Restaurant's

spare room. N. and I were out like lights. We woke to hear the
noise of mules champing about. Nikos and Alekkos had arrived
with all the remaining stuff and the day was spent by N. and me
very happily trying to think of somewhere to put them. Having
not a single receptacle for clothes as yet made for problems, so
suitcases were unpacked and repacked and we bumped into
each other throughout the day. 'Ah there you are,' we said to
each other cheerfully every time it happened. It was on our first
day in residence that one fact emerged with no shadow of a
doubt. I would have to Build On. To Spiti Mou was simply not
capacious enough to house two largish persons. However the
essential-comfort elements worked a treat. The beds were good
and soft, and the gas stove, operating on a cylinder which lasted
six weeks or so (a good twenty-five bob's worth), had three
rings which more than coped with the simple meals on which
we existed. The loo and the wash-basin tap both fulfilled their
functions as long as the mule remembered to bring the water up.

Nikos the Fisherman beetled off fairly soon as he had his own
Life to get on with and the season was about to start. But he kept
a constant and loving watch on us from Corfu and frequent
'boxes' of 'large fisses' and 'big meats' were sent over on the
ferry-boat, laced with fresh eggs, potatoes, and lemons from his
own home. We were never short of stuff though supplies in
Lakka at that time were pitifully sparse. Nikos always sent a note
and I knew that if we got into genuine trouble he'd pop over in
the *Athena*, dropping everything, including tourists, into the sea,
I fear.

It was difficult to keep the relationship from becoming entirely
one-sided. There was so little one could do to repay him. Apart
from the meticulous bills he presented via Mrs Vlachos, which
never included such things as labour or time spent on my
business, it was very dodgy trying to get money into his pocket.
The only way, I found by painful experiment, was to slip a tiny
bit in an envelope and say it was for Yorgos and Speroula. But
even with this I am under a huge debt to him. I know that it was
he who had to organize anyone to do anything and it is fiendish

work trying to recruit labour in Paxos. They are all picking, pruning or pressing olives or 'out fishing'. So I imagine it ended in him and Alekkos doing the lion's share on jobs like the new flopperoo water cistern about which far too much anon.

I simply cannot fathom the employment situation in Paxos. The olive crop occurs only once in two years and during that period everyone on the island works like a black. But in between whiles the young men go off to join the Merchant Navy (in 'sips' as they say) and the rest just seem to relax. If it were not for the excellence of the olive oil the island produces, it would be entirely dependent on Corfu for survival, as it is for the main part of its food and household supplies. But the Paxiots are a proud lot and consider themselves infinitely superior to the richer but betouristed Corfiotes. I know I do and I'm only one-eighth Paxiot. The inhabitants of the larger island make a lot of silly jokes about the people of Paxos. They say the natives are so simple that old ladies drop buckets down wells to catch the moon which has fallen down them. They also, it would appear, paint sardines yellow, put them in cages and expect them to sing. But the most elaborate fantasy the Corfiotes have devised is that once every few years the whole population of Paxos takes a large rope and puts it round Antipaxos and pulls on it in the hope that they will be able to join the two and make one big Paxos!

I view all these so-called 'jokes' as in the worst possible taste and never stop carrying on to my Corfiote friends about the peace and dignity of Paxos compared to the Sodom and Gomorrah-like character of Corfu. They also get pretty bored when I trot out my oft-repeated story from the historian Plutarch, relayed to me by that most delightful naturalist and microscopist, Dr Theodore Stephanides. Those of you who have read *My Family and Other Animals* will remember him well and realize the influence he had on Gerald Durrell's brilliant career. I don't mean Plutarch I mean Dr S., who has now lived in England for many years, and after a distinguished life devoted to medicine and study has retired to a tiny flat in Chelsea with (and I quote) 'some of the most beautiful and interesting things I have found in the last seventy-odd years'. I have had the privilege of seeing some of the slides and specimens he has collected over the years. It is to me regrettable that someone hasn't seized on Dr Stephanides as a potentially marvellous TV personality, who late at night would tell us what Life is all about. His war reminiscences and poems (both published in England) are full of sense and understanding.

Anyhow back to Plutarch! Who else for heaven's sake?

In an essay entitled 'The Obsolescence of Oracles' he describes an event said to have taken place during the reign of Tiberius (A.D. 14–37): 'A ship going to Italy was passing Paxos, when a loud voice called upon Thamus, the Egyptian pilot of the vessel, and told him to sail by Palodes (now Butrimo) opposite the north end of Corfu but on the mainland. As the voice came from nowhere and called him by name, Thamus was alarmed. The voice continued and ordered: "When you get there, tell them that Great Pan Is Dead!" '

Thamus sailed to Palodes and from off the shore repeated the phrase, 'GREAT PAN IS DEAD!' Whereupon there arose great cries of lamentation, 'not of one person but of many', which caused even more amazement to Thamus and the crew and passengers of the ship.

Plutarch himself (born *circa* A.D. 50) gives no explanation of this happening but some church commentators (so Dr Stephanides informed me) have read in it a presage of the passing of the old gods before the coming dawn of Christianity. The dates certainly fit and the legend has passed into history; the sentence 'Great Pan Is Dead' has been used many times, most notably in a poem by Oscar Wilde.

It's a thin thread for us Paxiots to hang on but it is easy to believe that, despite his death, the spirit of Pan still lingers on the island, and I tell those Corfiotes that there is more magic around Paxos than there ever was in their part of the Ionian. But they don't listen much and I have to admit that Corfu has had a fantastically interesting history. Few islands have had such a record of violence and change of ownership.

But to get back—if I may? Thanks—to Nikos Kaloudis, without whom none of it would have been possible. I think you may have formed the impression that I don't actually dislike him! To me he is that totally satisfactory kind of friend whose loyalty and love you need never doubt for a single second and who, you feel sure, will always be standing there with arms outstretched like a reassuring beacon. So what a shock it is when some physical misfortune overtakes him. Up till this year I had been convinced of his imperviousness to sickness or weakness, as he strikes one as a person to whom the Fates must be permanently kind. He has been endowed with an unbossy efficiency and self-discipline which influence his life. His handling of a craft is remarkable and he can do it all single-handed without moving a hair of those that are left on his dear head. Though his engine-room, or rather the *Athena*'s, is astern, he judges his approach to a jetty so expertly that he will get to the bows, jump ashore, tie up and be helping the customers ashore all in one long movement. During the months of July and August he works about twenty hours a day and snatches sleep when he can. His most profitable and most interesting trips are those that involve deep-sea fishermen or skin-divers who want someone to show them where the best places are. At week-ends he takes bathers and picnickers from the capital of Corfu, Kerkyra it is called by the Greeks, to the beaches of Dassia near his native village of Ypsos. They are about the best and safest in the area and, because the buses are inevitably and asphyxiatingly crammed, many people prefer to travel by caïque. Nikos does anything up to four or five voyages back and forth of a Sunday, and as he can take thirty to forty passengers at a time the financial rewards are not negligible.

He is usually accompanied by his son, Yorgos, who is one of the youngest first mates in the biz. But this period of plenty is very short as no Corfiote would dream of swimming till mid-June at the absolute earliest. Nikos also takes small coveys of tourists to Nisaki and Kassiopi, attractive small ports in the north of the island and only a few miles from the alarming shores of Albania. These are longish trips and involve a good deal of touting and organization. He does however have a motor-bike to get him to and from Corfu and on which he manages at a pinch to perch his entire family.

The last three Greek Easters I've spent with the Kaloudises have been beautiful. This year I couldn't get out early enough. I arrived some ten days late to be met at the airport by doe-eyed Hermione from Corfu Travel, a splendid firm who look after me, my mail and my friends. They also look after a good many other people too. On this cloudy cool day Hermione had some very bad news indeed. Nikos was in hospital in Athens, having smashed his hand up in an accident, helping someone else of course.

She handed me a very long letter from him written in Greek. On the envelope it had a message for Hermione to translate its contents. It was certainly the longest letter I had ever had from Nikos. It was written for him by his wife and the recurring motif was 'Very very very sorry. Work not finished on house. Soon to Come. Never Forget.' Nothing about his hand or his future and a complete absence of self-pity. Hermione finished reading the letter to me and I saw that she had tears in her eyes.

It was a terrible homecoming for me, because I knew apart from everything else we wouldn't have the fun we always have when Nikos tries to explain something new he has thought of and this year it was to be To Sterna (the cistern). The tangles we get into when mechanical matters are discussed have to be heard to be disbelieved.

Hermione told me that Nikki was coming into town the next day to 'explain everything'; Nikos had asked her to. When I got back to my hotel after a little light shopping I found her down in the lobby sitting with the two children and looking very smart. I had forgotten it was a Sunday and 'treat' day so we went into the bright streets and gave the children as many pasta and glyka (sweetmeats) as they could gorge. Nikki insisted that my Greek had improved and I did manage to glean the information from her that Nikos was improving and that he would be leaving hospital shortly. She went on about how distressed he was at the mess he'd left outside my house and how none of it was completed etc. I assured her of the unimportance of all this and said the only essential thing was that he should be made whole. What would become of all the family if Nikos was irreparably damaged? It didn't bear thinking about, as his living depends entirely upon superb health. There is not much of a pension scheme in Greece and I know that he would be far too proud to accept any form of charity. His family have never seemed to lack for anything and his generosity and hospitality are never-ending.

I left for Paxos disturbed but certain that he would somehow survive any misfortune. Two weeks later I got a note from him which just said 'Please to Come. If Possible. Much drinking. All good friends. Never Forget.'

On my next visit to Corfu I went out to Ypsos and walked across the fields to the little house where I have spent so very many happy hours. It is here that Nikos is in his element and immensely beguiling. All friends are welcome, large simple meals are produced from nowhere, and under his twinkling blue eyes and great capacity for enjoyment of life all language barriers vanish as glass after glass of wine disappears down his and everybody else's throat. The old jokes come trotting out and the children fall over themselves laughing. We pretend that the barbarones (evil spirits) have entered the house and are lurking under the table. This is achieved by judicious taps when the children aren't looking too closely. I am made to try to construct mice out of my handkerchief, which Master Finney did so successfully three Easters back; Yorgos counts up to eighty-three in English and suddenly gets bored; and Speroula does her imitation of Miss Samantha Eggar, on whom she dotes and who spent Greek Easter here with her husband Tom Stern a couple of years back; and Nikos tells for the umpteenth time, with eyes aglow, about the telegram he got from the Sterns saying they'd named their son Nikolas. All the old photos, letters and toys are brought out of the cupboard, most of them battered by use. In fact the whole evening was as usual except that the host had his arm in a sling and when he showed me the hurt it was really rather an alarming sight. One finger could not move at all and two others were pretty out of line. However Nikos just smiled though obviously constantly in pain.

'Slow-Slow, Mr Peter,' he said. 'Good soon. Much love for all company.' And it was extremely difficult not to blub in his face.

Weeks later the *Athena*, freshly painted and looking very smart indeed, came whirring into Lakka harbour. There was some frantic waving from the man at the tiller. When I got down to the port there was Nikos, his face aglow, his arm out of a sling, with a lot of tourists whom I suspect he'd dragged all the way to Paxos to show me his hand.

3. Bless This House

Nikos the Fisherman informed me that the Priest would be very happy to bless 'The Bullings'; I was enormously flattered and touched by Ho Pappas's kindness until I was told that it would cost eighty drachmae (about a pound or 2.78 dollars), fifty for himself and thirty for a yet unspecified but doubtless younger character who would swing the censer or whatever it was one swung at Blessings. Nikos's mime gave me no clue.

Now eighty drachs seemed quite a big sum to spend on blessing To Spiti Mou. You do realize, don't you, that I must write in phonetic Greek because my typewriter, for some obscure reason, doesn't seem to have any hellenic lettering. And for all I know this might apply to Hazel, Watson and Viney, or Morrison and Gibb, or whichever firm of Messrs may be printing this load of rubbish.

Anyhow at that time 'To Spiti Mou' was about the only phrase that I was able to string together, apart from 'Thello na martho Hellenika' (I want to learn Greek), which, repeated for the fourth time to the same person, is apt to bring a look of cynical exasperation into the kindest of soft eyes.

On the other hand it must be confessed that words for food came readily to my tongue and I could achieve actual possession of 'psohmee' (bread) and 'krema caramelle' (cream caramel) in next to no time, to say nothing of 'sygonarki', a Greek welsh rarebit which I think Ulysses must have been quite glad to get his molars into after one of those interminable journeys.

All this linguistic knowledge of mine was significant of the lusts of the flesh, I fear, because the moment I needed a screwdriver, a clothes peg or a tractor, I was reduced to behaving like a gibbering lunatic, gesticulating and making faces which could have qualified me for the nearest institution.

All this hasn't much to do with The Blessing. I do see that. But I am coming back to it, I promise. Slightly shocked by the commercial aspect of the affair I discussed it with Nikos the Fisherman—Ho Phillos Mou. This expression, which means 'My Friend', has never been more beautifully apt but I've been into all that before. (See page one. You must have got that far.) Anyhow I suggested to him that perhaps there might be a reduction because of the size of the building but he told me reprovingly that there were no cut rates where the Greek Orthodox Church was concerned.

Mark you, I am pretty keen on the G.O.C. myself and think their services are smashing. There is also an informality about the atmosphere in their churches during non-service times which is particularly impressive. People pop in on their way to shop, work or to see friends and stay a while to gossip. There is always a gentle Pappas around to give advice or cheer and in the great church of St Spiridion, where the saint himself lies contentedly (we hope) in a beautiful silver casket, the scene is most moving. There appears to be none of that constant nagging for alms, which almost destroys any religious feelings one has on entering a church building. My favourite place in the whole of Corfu is a tiny twelfth century Byzantine chapel which lies on the outskirts of the town. Here you can roam about or just sit quietly in the cool of the old stone without anyone disturbing you. Outside there is a wonderful wild garden and the whole feeling is unique. Yet it is a very poor church and I imagine badly in need of money for restoration.

So, feeling as I did about the Greek Orthodox Church, I was determined to have the Blessing but felt impelled to mention to Nikos certain indisputable facts. For instance, it would only cost me eighty drachmae to stay for a week in the capital city at a hotel called Beautiful Greece, where they give guests showers in the foyer, if they ask for them. The resulting floods, nearly up to reception-desk level, cause a bit of inconvenience to the other residents. Contrariwise a week here, in possibly Unhiltonian luxury, can be endured for just over eighty drachmae.

Nikos said that he saw my point but did I really want to spend a week under the roofs of Beautiful Greece, and he added, in I thought a slightly sinister way, would it not be wiser to have To Spiti Mou blessed than cursed? This was of course unanswerable. We were already having trouble with To Meros (the water closet) which, though undoubtedly the Wonder of the Village, was not getting through its second week of existence without a peculiar cacophony of groans and splutters. It was obvious that Cursing it wasn't going to help any and a Blessing might perk it up.

Incidentally it's curious how one's friends react when one mentions casually that one has built a house in Greece. They never say 'Oh, how divine!', 'Clever you' or even 'You must be MAD'. No, they just stare at one in a supercilious and pitying way and ask what one intends to use for sanitary arrangements and assert that one is Bound to have Trouble with One's Water. In actual fact the first two years the water came whizzing up once a day on Alekkos's mule. If the latter could be persuaded to stand still long enough, it was then decanted from the petrol cans and poured into the Main Water System, an old oil-barrel painted maroon. Then the Magic started. If the water was reaching a high enough level, To Meros flushed divinely, and no sound could be sweeter than the bobbing of the ball-cock, if you will forgive the phrase. And of course you have no option because the new censorship permits me to use it with impunity. Dear old imp Unity.

I will now admit that the water situation did cause a good many problems but not, and this is the point I've been trying to make, in the way One's Friends intimated it would. It did cost a great deal of money to keep things fluid but the liquid was always obtainable. And I did find that the runaway basin did tempt the extravagant guest to leave a Tap Running, which to my Paxiot eyes seemed a rather more serious crime than clubbing an old crippled lady to death. Yet it was difficult to remonstrate a few minutes after a guest's arrival in the house. On the other hand perhaps it would have been better than Atmosphering, and Lurking in the Runaway Basin area. At that time To Meros and the Runaway B. took up nearly half the house. The Bed-Sitting Room took up the remaining space and for once the phrase was dead accurate. There were two beds and That was the Sitting-Room. All the chairs had to be kept outside so as to make room for sitting down inside. Get the picture?

At the outset I knew I would have to buy a gigantic wardrobe to store everything, owing to the fact that the words 'chest of drawers' seem to be extinct or taboo in this part of the world. I could foresee that the additional piece of furniture, however svelte, would immediately create a Bed Standing-Room but at least it would get us off our stomachs, where we seemed to spend quite a lot of time grovelling for handkerchiefs, shirts, band-aids and Scrabble tiles.

All this preamble is to show you that it did appear advisable to invoke outside aid wherever possible and on the eighth day of our residency Ho Pappas was due to honour the building. We spent most of the morning (N. and I) trying to decide (a) what to wear and (b) what to serve in the way of refreshment. We came to the conclusion that, having only one sober tie between us, we would have to dress slightly informally, though we would wear shoes. The drink problem was far more dodgy. It narrowed down to ouzo and/or turcico (Greek coffee) as the only permissible alternatives and we found that we had no equipment in the house for serving either. So I sped down to the village to buy some dwarf glasses and coffee cupettes.

I must say I find it hard to believe that once there were great godlike creatures peopling Greece; and even, at a slightly more conservative assessment, drawings and paintings show the inhabitants as being at least of normal stature. Things seem very different nowadays and every single commodity seems to have been Munchkinized to the point of lunacy. (Lilliputted for those who never saw or read *The Wizard of Oz*.) From mattresses to coffee-cups the midget is superbly catered for but heaven help the six-footer in bed of a winter evening and running severe risk of frostbite.

This is a National problem, not that they treat it as one, though I would have thought it has become International as a result of the surging tourist traffic, but at least it has nothing to do with the blessing of To Spiti Mou.

I washed my newly-acquired cups and glasses (seemingly blown for your average-sized fairy) and, come to think of it, my face, which I then buried in the Greek-English phrase book. I was beginning to get very windy indeed and hurried to the section devoted to Difficulties. But, alas and alack, the author did not appear to have foreseen the possibility of their arising out of the Blessing of Houses. In restaurants, hotels, buses, post offices, dentists' and hairdressers' one was catered for superbly. Yes indeedy, but phrases like 'How much should I tip the maid?' or 'I part my hair on the other side' were unlikely to demonstrate to Ho Pappas our worthiness to be Blessed. I decided to play it by ear and not mouth and content myself with occasionally emitting an 'epharisto' (F. Harry Stowe). This means 'thank you'.

Zero hour (1700 hours) came and not a sign of the expected cavalcade up the hill. N. and I sat in what amounted to our Kyriakee kalitero (Sunday best) not daring to beat the daylights out of a new bottle of ouzo. We thought that Ho Pappas might think we were just a couple of Atheist Alcoholics if he caught us imbibing before To Spiti Mou had been blessed for such excesses.

Finally, when we'd almost given up hope and N.'s hand was on the bottle, we heard voices and the Priest hove into view, followed by Alekkos, my factotum. It was obvious that the latter was about to essay a new role, and though he was not everybody's idea of a censer-swinger it was he who was to assist Ho Pappas through the ceremony. He was dispatched, after the welcoming pleasantries, to fetch various props. These included some olive leaves, a glass of water, and a discarded tile from the roof on which to place four charcoal cones of incense, which Ho Pappas withdrew from his garments. He (H.P.) then took his tall hat off, revealing an almost snow-white forehead over a deep brown and rather beautiful face, added a vestment, put his hat on again and we were off. Even before he had taken out his prayer book he started intoning. At the same time he placed the glass of water on our only upright chair and leaned a small wooden cross against it. Then he raised his hands to heaven, and in reply to a seraphic nod from Alekkos, we stationed ourselves behind him.

The ceremony was naturally incomprehensible to the entire congregation of two and I rather suspect that even Alekkos didn't know the form all that well. He muffed several of the responses and, when apparently lost for an answer, muttered words that sounded like the Greek equivalent of 'rhubarb rhubarb'.

After quite a long stretch of dialogue Ho Pappas lit the pieces of charcoal and an even stronger pong than usual permeated the little room. Suddenly there was an explosion when the tile cracked and for a moment I feared for The Chair, which had pretty plastic strands across its dear little bottom. But after a bit of back-chat and smiles of reassurance the Blessing went smoothly on. Till this point we had taken little or no part in the service beyond crossing ourselves to please Alekkos who was crossing himself like a pair of excessively active knitting needles. But to our surprise Ho Pappas suddenly leaned down, dipped the olive leaves in the toothglass, wheeled round and sprinkled some drops of water on our foreheads. We kissed his cross and embarked on a tour of the building.

He splashed the whitewashed walls of the Bed-Sitting Room, entered our kitchen and after giving that a good going-over proceeded, to our huge delight and relief, to spend a good time in the loo, swishing and sprinkling with the utmost abandon. After that we shuffled back into the B.S.R. for the closing part of the ceremony. Ho Pappas took up his stance again and had a certain amount of difficulty in reading the name of the house he was blessing. I had written it as clearly as possible on an old airmail envelope. But 'The Bullings' is something to challenge any Greek from the outset as their B turns into a V without so much as a by-your-leave, and to make the English B sound, they have to impose an MP (as in MPOULL which is how they normally spell my name). I knew there was going to be troubola at the post office, etc. when I arrived, which was one of the reasons why I had repeated the name in 'The Mpoullings'. Anyhow Ho Pappas staggered through (it sounded like 'Vullink' actually) and turned to us; we shook hands and I pressed eighty drachmae into his palm. Then we offered refreshment, which he and Alekkos refused. There was a good deal of frantic signalling from the latter around this period, as if I was about to embark on a series of social gaffes, but after a lot of smiling and making noises of the most friendly nature our guests started down the hill.

Later that day, as we sat sipping ouzo in the seemingly warm moonlight, the house suddenly did appear more complete. The windows and door looked more like a face than ever and looking around we realized that the fireflies dancing attendance on us were legion. We had indeed been Blessed.

4. *My Feud with Mr Ypsilos*

It is singularly unfortunate that the only person in the village, or indeed entire island, with whom I continually cross swords should be my landlord, Kyrios Ypsilos. No, perhaps 'landlord' isn't the right word but he's the man who sold me the land on which I built my house and he owns all the surrounding area and behaves as if he also had proprietary rights over my property.

I have no fences or gates and he tends to come up without any warning and at the most inappropriate time. It drives me frantic, not that he offers violence or sets fire to the place. It's just the way he walks over MY land and looks at MY olive-trees. He has a very strong personality and is not unlike what might happen if General de Gaulle were to marry Jacques Tati and have issue. He is enormously tall, which makes him appear a giant among his fellow Greeks, and he has rather distinguished hair, which as I said earlier, ends on his forehead in some curious pink disease of the skin with an accompanying carbuncle (or carbaunt) of a not wildly attractive nature. It is as if his very strong temper had erupted silently and in protest. Many's the time I've seen him burst into a sudden rage over a game of cards or backgammon in the café.

I must admit that when I first met him I thought he was

rather a dear. This meeting I have described at some length in the first chapter and I don't intend to subject you to all that again. Rich fruity prose has never been my forte (well, what has for goodness sake?) and I try to press on to something ridiculous, droll or plain loony. However every now and again I have to Face Facts, a situation I frankly don't enjoy. But it's possible that you skipped the first chapter and started this book half-way and so in order to help you and make it remotely comprehensible I have to State or Restate Facts. The Fact was that I bought the land, or rather Nikos the Fisherman did, and before I left Paxos at the end of that trip arrangements were concluded for Kyrios Ypsilos to come to Corfu to sign a lot of legal documents.

The next stage in negotiations was his advent. He arrived at the hotel where I was staying, with his seemingly anarchical grandchild, who attempted to break anything in sight, from the hotel swing-doors to his grandfather's spirit. Kyrios Y. had brought me a huge bunch of flowers which he just managed to keep out of the dear little boy's reach by holding it over his head. Their entrance and stay not unnaturally caused a sensationette in the usually orderly San Rocco Hotel. I was touched by the thought however and quite forgot that old saying about bewaring of Greeks bearing gifts. We adjourned to the lawyer's with Nikos the Fisherman and that in itself was a fascinating experience. I don't know if it's the same all over Greece but in Corfu the offices are open for all and sundry to pop in, listen or just have a jolly good sit-down. In fact they look exactly like shops. All the counters, so to speak, had customers so we sat on seats in a sort of Musical Chairs type queue. Eventually we found ourselves facing a nice kindly gent with a hearing-aid. After a short parley with him it was disclosed that Mr Ypsilos had omitted to bring with him not only the vital papers for any transaction but any papers at all. As we had paid for his passage back and forth this did not bode frightfully well for our business relationship.

It was imperative to study Mr Ypsilos's documents to see what the olive-tree situation was. Unless one is exceptionally careful, one can be plagued for a lifetime by having bought a

piece of land with an olive-tree on it which belongs to some other party or is a portion of a dowry promised to some young lady. In the latter case it would mean that she could uproot it and take it wherever she wanted to, or, far more likely, just go harping on about it being HERS, and squatting under it from time to time, which might make any social intercourse one was contemplating at the time a tidge etsi-ketsi ('dodgy', but you must know that one by now).

So Mr Ypsilos was dispatched back to Paxos to fetch the necessary papers. Additional funds were provided and I told him that next time I saw him I wanted to see something else in his hands besides his grandchild. A few days later he came back, apparently with the genuine stuff, and all was signed, sealed and delivered. Nikos and I went quietly ahead with our plans for the house and the following spring I returned to Paxos to find The Bullings a *fait accompli*. I was fully prepared for further tralala from Mr Ypsilos as Nikos had warned me that he was not the most restful and placid of men. So it was no surprise to me to find that he was fully convinced that I would go on buying more bits of land from him *ad infinitum*. He was also sure that every visitor to my house was probably an American millionaire, who would form a business association with him, Mr Ypsilos, and enable him and Mrs Y. to live in luxury for the rest of their lives. And certainly to provide his grandchild with enough toys to smash up from day to day.

One of the consequences of his theory was that not only did Mr Ypsilos meet every ferry-boat, but, if it happened to carry any friend of mine as a passenger, he offered himself immediately as a porter. My astonished chums, if not previously warned, would blench at the extraordinary sight of this gaunt Greek inclining his great height in a gesture of subservience. And then, if I was not nippy enough to forestall him, a terrible tug-of-war would ensue between him and me for possession of the luggage. Quite accurately he assumed that possession was nine-tenths of the law and if this was achieved it would enable him to start selling land to the unsuspecting guest before he or she had had time to sit down. As his English was non-existent the flow of gibberish bewildered and frightened the hapless listener. So in order to smooth things over I would have to carry on a reassuring commentary: 'The old sod's trying to flog his land to you. Don't pay any attention. He'll go away soon,' etc. etc.

One of the great mysteries of life to me is the way so many people automatically assume that one wants to live encircled by friends. Perhaps I'm kinky but dearly as I love so many people, and I can smugly and safely say that I am permanently warmed by their love, I prefer them to be at least a mile away so that (a) one appreciates them even more and (b) one doesn't get claustro-phobia. And leave us face it, if one has chosen one of the more remote Greek islands to settle in, it's loony to suppose that one would like the area to be turned into a sort of hellenic King's Road, Chelsea.

But Mr Ypsilos is certain that every one of my visitors is going to construct a house within speaking distance of The Bullings, and nothing will dispel this fantasy. One can with luck delay the bargaining lunge by wresting the visitors' luggage away from him before he has got to the foot of the hill. His stamina is not all that hot, and if one can hurry one's party along he does tend to get a bit flustered, and while he's struggling for breath I can sometimes give a great tug which, combined with a slight push, will nonplus him. I smile bewitchingly at old Ypsilos and thank him, at the same time issuing instructions to the guest(s) to whip up the hill as quickly as poss. They are so startled that they comply at breakneck speed, convinced that the Mafia are involved.

But one's troubles are not over by any means, even if this ploy succeeds, because later in the day, when Mr Y. has recovered his strength, his gaunt figure will appear over the brow of the hill, practically always when one is about to serve a complicated and elaborate meal involving dishes from all parts of the property, i.e. the barbecue at one end of The Terrace, the stove in The Cuisine and the fridge in The Bedroom (natch). I always try to serve newcomers with a spiffing and appetizing meal their first evening to offset the undoubted primitiveness in other departments.

I therefore resent it deeply if Mr Ypsilos times his arrival to coincide with the figurative gong. It's a moot point whether he plans this but he certainly provides a carbuncled skeleton at the feast. Following the example of the fantastic hospitality I have received from the Greeks I always offer him a glass of something, however livid I am. This he refuses, pointing to his stomach and suggesting nameless diseases which do not apparently prevent him from eating one out of house and home.

Having not catered for him as a possible dinner guest, I hand him alternative goodies and he hardly finishes the last of the *petit-beurres* (little-butters) before he starts carrying on about His Land. My poor guests are eventually forced to look at the property behind the house, which gets them out of doing the washing-up but otherwise has no merit as an action. Neither party understands a word the other says and I leave them to it. Although an impasse is always reached there are, it must be confessed, several distinct advantages in letting him carry on the way he does.

All through the spring and summer the old thing believes there is a reasonable hope of a prospective buyer arriving from London, New York, or indeed Nether Wallop, but at the end of my yearly visit, when nothing has materialized, his enforced abandonment of hope is, I fear, a grievous shock to his system. It is then that I am able, with the help of Nikos the Fisherman, to bargain for the extra land I need to enlarge my holding. Every year I lay my hands on a few more square yards. The trouble is, the moment I've done this he is up like a whippet to see that I haven't gone beyond the boundary lines. As I tend to put articles of furniture, clothes-lines, barbecues and assorted paraphernalia all over the joint, it all gets a bit moot. To Sterna (the water-tank) that is now installed stretches a few feet outside My Land, Mr Ypsilos maintains, and it's no good trying to soften his heart by telling him that at least the danger of warts has been averted. You see, water which has been used for boiling eggs is supposed to cause warts if used on the face or I imagine on other parts of the anatomy.

Owing to the scarcity of the liquid, I have been tending to disguise the eggy water and dish it out to unsuspecting guests. I do take a peek at them from time to time afterwards to see if their warts (if any) have increased. Now, since the water-tank's arrival, the lucky flowers get it which they certainly prefer to the washing-up water.

In order to build To Sterna it was necessary to negotiate for additional territory, and the moment that Mr Ypsilos realized he had the whiphand he became a different person and waited quietly for us to go cap in hand. Nikos the Fisherman managed it, as always, superbly, but Mr Y. thought he'd done very well out of us. Perhaps he had and it is certainly his favourite type of situation. I personally think my coming to Paxos has revolutionized his life and put fresh ditto into him. He is an ex-policeman, and a long sojourn on the peaceful and apparently largely lawabiding island must have been frightfully boring for him. I know that for the first few weeks after our arrival he followed us into every store, poked his great fingers into every shopping-basket, examined both the incoming and outgoing mail and generally nearly drove us out of our minds. If I were more charitable I suppose I would make more allowances for his behaviour and realize that to him Nelson and I looked such an unlikely pair of residents as to warrant his keeping the tabs on us on behalf of Interpol. But whereas to the rest of the village we were a seven days' wonder, to Mr Ypsilos we were a seventy-seven days' ditto. In fact the other inhabs suddenly stopped peering and prying, and overnight (during the fortnightly film festival in the café as it turned out) managed to convey delicately that we were now part of the community. Mr Ypsilos on the other hand intensified his third-degree scrutiny of our daily life.

For a long time we somehow managed to keep him out of the interior of To Spiti Mou. He had been dying to get in and have a jolly good dekko but Nelson and I always contrived to forestall his entry by rushing out and drawing him down to the terrace on some excuse or other but one far more valid than those he had come armed with to disturb us of a morning. Mark you, as my dear mother used to say, he had every right to survey his own property, but not, I maintain, to do so from mine. The barbecue and various other improvements have definitely infringed on his land and luckily he doesn't notice them much. But anything that involves moving huge bits of stone from one place to another is spotted immediately by his beady eye. Most of the new construction work has been organized by N., who for an artistic gent has remarkable talent as a handy-man. He also revolutionized the draining system connected with the Runaway Basin which hadn't frankly Run Away quite enough and had started to offend his delicate nostrils. And this was when Mr Ypsilos's 'petra' (rocks) started to disappear from the cliff edge. They were used to build up a huge fortification to stop the upsurge of the runaway basin's rejects. We simply didn't dare go into the question of where other waste went, mentioning no names, but the initials are W.C. What I have always dreaded is that That is likely to come to the surface and pop up under the dining area or somewhere equally convenient. Whenever I ask Nikos the Fisherman or Alekkos about the Loo Disposal Location, they keep their eyes averted and infer that the 'thalassa' (sea) takes care of it all. I find this an improbable solution but am too petrified to pursue the subject further. *Che sarà sarà* (What will be, will be) as dear old Dame Doris Day used to sing.

Anyhow the great thing on Mr Ypsilos's visits was to give him no chance to have a jolly good look round and to keep him fully occupied. The best way to achieve this was to put a whole tin of mixed biscuits into his hand and steer him towards the edge of the cliff, though contriving to refrain at the last moment from pushing him over. We further ingratiated ourselves by offering him a tin of fairly nasty 'marmelada' (jam, surprisingly) which we had been misled by pretty pictures into thinking was lovely fruit. Mr Ypsilos used to spread it so thickly on his biccies that they collapsed from the weight and he had to catch the mess as it fell.

The basic trouble with Mr Y. is that in a non-olive producing year he has nothing to occupy himself with from cock-crow till dusk, when he goes on a backgammon jag to Spiro's Café. Here he bangs his pieces about unmercifully and shouts at his opponents. I only hope he doesn't cheat as much at other games as he does at Gin Rummy. N. and I made the mistake of taking our cards downtown one night and embarking on a game. Mr Ypsilos zoomed over from the café across the road (Nikolaus's) as if under hypnosis, and stationed himself behind us, breathing heavily. We were in the middle of a game when he suddenly grabbed the cards and we were playing a three-handed job before either of us could say 'Gin' or even 'Ouzo'. The most infuriating part of it all was that he won the very first game but only by peering over our cards from his great height. He was thus Helped to Victory but in a not frightfully endearing way. So we had to resort to Scrabble but I'm sure he'll have a bash at that before long, even if he doesn't understand one single English word.

I am afraid I'm not painting a very attractive portrait of my landlord (so to speak) but I assure you he is Mr Perfect compared to what his dear little grandchild was when Mr Y. brought him up to see us on his visits to Paxos. The kiddiwink did more damage in ten minutes than the stampede of goats to which we are occasionally subjected. On his last foraging expedition he contrived to upset three tins of paint, a barrel of whitewash and both the occupants of To Spiti Mou. Finally, seeing there was no chance of their leaving in the immediate future, we barricaded ourselves inside the house, pretending we had had a sudden and unexpected attack of leprosy. Peering through the shutters we watched the spooky pair encamp just below us, as if they were intent on proving squatters' rights or something.

But these joint forays were mercifully rare and even Mr Ypsilos seemed to get tired of the steep climb, though I think a hintette was dropped from the right quarter that one wasn't mad about his haunting the area. In the village too we found that by dodging behind buildings as if we were playing Grandmother's Steps we were able to shop unattended in a satisfactory though disjointed way. True he did seem to dog us in Corfu one trip.

We had gone to assist the new young King of Greece celebrate the Centenary of the Union of Corfu with the Ionian Islands and the whole lot's freedom from the British Protectorate. We had gone to celebrate also our supposed freedom from Mr Ypsilos. But he was of course a fellow-passenger on the ferry-boat, sharing our lunch uninvited, drawing attention to N.'s few grey hairs and making himself generally a bit of a nuisance to the captain, all the mates and most of the voyagers on the good ship *Aspasia*.

In the crowds that thronged Corfu for the occasion we thought we were bound to lose him but, oh no, goodness me no, there he was at one's side when one least expected him. Even as the King passed us in his processional parade there was Mr Ypsilos, appearing as if by magic or summoned by a genie and making insane noises down one's neck. And when N. sneaked off to the Kinematograph to see *Attila the Hun* who should be waving wildly at him in the intermission but that tall spectral form? Where would it all end? That's what we asked ourselves. And for the life of me I can't remember what we answered ourselves. But Mr Ypsilos, thrilled by the regal goings-on, stayed on in the capital for a bit and we had a gorgeous short respite.

However it was too good to last and one morning (8.30 ack emma actually) there I was typing some rubbish on this machine (well, not this one but the one before) when I saw to my horror Mr Ypsilos advancing on me to the *terrazza*. Breathing heavily, he carried an as yet unidentifiable object in his hands. On closer inspection (under my nose in fact) it proved to be a live lobster, which even in its comparatively parlous state of captivity was managing to get in some sharpish nips at Mr Y.'s arms. The whole operation, I realized subsequently, was a fresh bid to get inside the house. I was at a loss for words and could only manage 'Tee aurea' (How lovely!), a remarkably silly comment, as a more dodgy and alarming creature it would be impossible to imagine, always excepting Mr Ypsilos's grandson of course. Recovering my composure slightly, and smelling a rat, I surmised that the lobster was unlikely to be a present from a grateful landlord.

'Poso;' (How much?) I inquired. You think there ought to be a ? after 'Poso', don't you, and either the printers or I have made an error! Well, that's just where you are wrong, so sucks! And, if you thought you'd caught us out in the middle of p. 28, double sucks! That sort of thing at school always ended with 'Anyhow you smell', didn't it? But I wouldn't dream of saying that to you, gentle reader. The fact remains that the Greeks don't use question marks but semi-colons to express the interrogative. So heaven knows what happens when one NEEDS a semi-colon.

So I asked 'Poso' (semi-colon) in my most business-like manner and I thought he replied five drachmae, which seemed reasonable enough, being one and threepence in English money or under twenty cents in American. I gave him the money, which he looked at scornfully, nearly dropping the lobster. There was apparently a misunderstanding and the price was fifty drachmae. I decided to take the great beast (it would make a change from the corned beef anyhow) and it was worth buying if only for the simple reason that it was the only one of those present (Nelson had joined us for the bargaining) who had actually bitten Mr Ypsilos.

'So far,' said N. in a rather sinister way.

Anyhow I gave the old man a Greek bank-note and two biscuits with their full quota of marmelada on them and returned to my typewriter after thanking him and saying goodbye. To my secret amazement he started for the path down the hill. Five minutes later I looked round instinctively and there he was breathing down my neck and looking spooky. He must have gone round to the back of the house, where fortunately there is no entrance. He said goodbye again, the second of five he was to dish out periodically during the next half-hour. As he started to shuffle off he cast a wistful eye at the interior of the house, where N. was pretending to be deeply immersed in creative art of an all-absorbing type. At that moment my radio, which I thought I'd turned off, clocked in with some rather soothing and melodic programme. Mr Ypsilos came straight back and studied the machine with intermittent grunts and snorts. He switched stations and touched off a hysterical bazooka-type concert, which is one of the few accompaniments to which I find it impossible to type.

Though hardly able to keep my hands off him, I flashed him a terrifying smile, which caused him to make another exit. I started to try to work again until I caught sight of Nelson out of the corner of my eye issuing cautiously from the house, believing that our late guest-landlord had gone. Not a bit of it. With a swift lolloping gait and from apparently nowhere Mr Ypsilos reappeared, pounced on N. and the next I saw of them was sitting side by side in embarrassed silence on the rocks by the cliff face.

Finally Mr Y., after waving and beaming at me in an unusually inane way, got up, and instead of taking the road down to the village set off in the opposite direction, which even he must have known had no future at all, leading as it does only to a practically perpendicular descent to the sea. N. and I gave up after this, our respective creating mornings spoilt, and waited for his next move. Twenty minutes later he passed by the terrace where N. was lying reading. The front door was open and for once unguarded. Mr Ypsilos was in like a whippet and that was that. We couldn't get him out till he had given it a real once-over. Merry as a grig and talking rapid incomprehensible Greek, he appeared to be giving us colourful advice about flies, lobsters and, I think, life. Finally he disappeared, happy and relaxed.

In a few hours the entire village would know the colour of the bed-covers, how many tins of ham reposed on the shelves and what sort of toothpaste we used. But who cared? Not us. We just laughed at his retreating and indomitable figure and went to look at the lobster which had caused all this commotion. We found it in the long grass, bearing the contented, resigned look of one who has died valiantly in action.

Since this incident Mr Ypsilos has brought no gifts to To Spiti Mou but it has become increasingly difficult to ignore his presence. There is no denying his powerful personality and I sense that for many years he has had a strong influence on the local inhabs. He is certainly one of the leading olive negotiators and I have seen him presiding at meetings, where ugly scenes are the rule rather than the exception. It is difficult to assess his popularity with the village but it is obvious that our joke-feud is found highly enjoyable. I think he has probably bullied some of the weaker fry and I do get a lot of support. The population realized very early on that I was having 'difficulties' in our relationship and I decided to use some pretty unorthodox methods to gain sympathy. Greeks adore feuds and even very old people take a childish delight in watching two people having a row. I started my campaign by pretending to be terrified of Mr Ypsilos. I used to hide behind street corners if I heard that he was in the vicinity. I would then whisper and point, overacting the whole thing quite hideously. After one or two of these performances I was assured of a large and co-operative audience and both young and old entered into the spirit of the thing and followed my antics with avid delight. There were several variations; the one that had the biggest success was the Sudden Confrontation scene. This usually occurred after a prolonged game of Hide-and-Seek when, as if by error but actually contrived to a second, I would find myself face to face with Mr Ypsilos. I would then greet him with astonishing cordiality and *bonhomie* beyond the bounds of probability. I would end by slapping him on the back with a ferocity which practically knocked him flat.

When my Greek improved slightly and I was able to have short bouts of conversation with some of the residents, I still pretended I could not understand a single word Mr Y. was saying. I was always pretty certain it was something about money and/or buying more land and I didn't dare get involved without the aid of Nikos the Fisherman. But my dumbness did frustrate Mr Ypsilos beyond his powers of endurance and he started to fight back in his own way. Whenever he conceivably could he tried to time his trips to and from Corfu to coincide with mine, in the secret hope that he might catch Nikos and me together and force us to give him some money. I used to try to find out what day he was planning on and go a day later. On one occasion I did this and went down to the jetty to see the boat off; I saw Mr Ypsilos's pinkish eyes light up at my approach with a suitcase. But it was empty, and I waited till they were slipping and jumped off. The next day when I got to Corfu I did run slap into him on the big square. He greeted me rather ebulliently and told me that Nikos had gone that day to Paxos. As I'd come over from there entirely to see Nikos I was pretty livid. It wasn't till far later in the day when I saw Nikos in Ypsos that I realized Mr Y. had been, Having Me On. He had indeed started paying me back in my own coin and on my return to Paxos after a trip he'd surprise me by not being on the jetty to greet the ferry-boat. (It was his custom to meet her daily to keep the tabs on incoming prospective prospectors.) I would get off the machine with my luggage and a lot of parcels containing new excitements for the house or the stomach and, just as I was arranging with Alekkos for their distribution as regards mules, backs, hands or humping, Mr Ypsilos would surface and offer to help. This meant that even before one had said 'Okki' (No) he would be poking everything within sight, trying to guess the contents of every package. I used to lie copiously, telling him they were bombs or fireworks, but I'm afraid this was no more accepted than my explanation as to where I had been. If I had a cut or a swollen face I used to tell him that I'd received them fighting in Albania. I would mime popping noises or actually make them if it was something other than the face that was swollen. It is one of my more successful parlour tricks and will keep a reasonably normal kiddiwink interested for quite a time. Mr Ypsilos's great moonface would study my serious one for a long time and he would pretend to believe everything I told him, until he sensed the grinning onlookers and then he'd join in with a jolly forced laugh. But the whole of our relationship has become part of the life of the village and everyone, including the protagonists, enjoys it all hugely.

If he decides to go to Corfu, at least a dozen people make it their business to inform me of the fact. When I ask them the date of his return they tell me and wait happily for the pay-off. For, having ascertained the date, I intimate that THAT is the day

on which I will be leaving for Corfu. We shall pass in the middle
of the sea. 'Tee kreema!' (What a pity!) I say with a tragic look.
And they very kindly and indulgently shriek with laughter.

My association with Mr Ypsilos is kept within bounds because
I leave all the business side of our dealings entirely in the capable
hands of Nikos the Fisherman. During the winter following my
first residential summer a deal involving the sale of some extra
land was negotiated. It included some olive-trees and an area
large enough to build the guest-room. The day following my
return to Paxos I went down to the village to kiss and hug
everyone within reason. I left Nikos and Alekkos on the terrace
working out sums. My reception by the good people of Lakka
was super and I savoured the additional delight of it being
Ypsilos-free. I started back up the hill but as I rounded the school-
house I felt instinctively that I was being followed and turned to
find that well-known white-haired character in hot pursuit. I
greeted him warmly but not too so, as I disengaged myself
gingerly from his grasp. He indicated that he was coming up to
To Spiti Mou, and though I tried to dissuade him I was fighting
a lost cause.

Half-way up the hill we ran into somebody with whom Mr
Ypsilos started to have a row and I used the opportunity to press
on with a curt 'Andio' (Goodbye) knowing perfectly well that it
wouldn't have the slightest effect on him. But the incident did
enable me to reach my chums several minutes before our uninvited guest. There was unfortunately no drawbridge to pull up
and we had to rely on the simple ploy of Action Stations. In due
course a panting but totally undaunted figure came round the
corner. Alekkos and Nikos went quietly on with their arithmetic
and I stood over them. Mr Ypsilos took the most comfortable
chair and watched them with intense curiosity. They tried to hide
the figures from his merciless eyes but it was a formidable task.
Suddenly he interrupted them with a flood of conversation, and
gestures which included frequent pointings at me. Nikos just
stared blankly at him. There was a long pause and I looked
inquiringly at Nikos.

'Mr Ypsilos wants to know if you want to buy the rocks,' he announced.

'Which ones?' I asked.

'Those.'

I studied the small stone wall to which he pointed and realized how frightfully silly Mr Y. was being. The 'rocks' were at the far side of my terrace and just beyond them was a more or less sheer drop into the sea. It was fairly obvious to anyone in his right mind that nobody, except possibly a modern Icarus, would fancy building a house there. For those without Classical Educations, Icarus and his dad, Daedalus, flew with wings from Crete to escape the wrath of the king and poor old Icarus went too near the sun, which melted his wings so that he fell plop into the sea. But the point I'm trying to make is that the bit of property Mr Ypsilos was trying to flog me would have done quite well for them as a jumping-off place.

Anyhow I told Nikos I wasn't interested in buying those particular rocks, kind as it was of Mr Y. to think of little me. Mr Y. was clearly put out and started to get cross with Alekkos because his (Alekkos's) mule was eating one of his (Mr Ypsilos's) olive-trees. I didn't like to point out to him that he (Mr Ypsilos) had just demolished the last of the mixed biscuits (mine) that I'd left carelessly on the table for my two financial advisers.

After a long survey of the visitor, Nikos turned to me. 'Him old man,' he said in English with a charming smile. 'Dead very soon.'

He returned to his accounts and I helped myself to a large ouzo. I was quite saddened by what Nikos had just said. I realized that, if something did happen to that ridiculous character, something quite irreplaceable would disappear from my island life. I would regret it genuinely and sincerely. People larger than life appear to be getting fewer and farther between and I'm really rather fond of the old buzzard. (I might learn eventually not to have such a distaste for his destructive grandson.) He must have many stalwart points as his wife and family are very good people indeed. If only he'd leave one alone and not go on

66

so much. He must know that I shall never make a decision of any importance on my own on Greek soil.

In a few months' time, after I've left and all hope of selling plots of land, rocks, olive-trees or even olive oil to my mythically wealthy visitors has evaporated, Nikos will quietly buy the next bit of land that I lust after. And I needn't lift a finger. Poor Mr Ypsilos!

5. A Night at the Movies

Very early on during my first summer in Lakka I went down one day to buy some tins of sardines and was fairly astonished to see a lot of faded film stills outside the grocer's shop. On closer inspection they turned out to be of a film called *The Prince of Thieves* starring Jon Hall and Patricia Morrison. I hastened up the hill to tell N. the glad news. He hadn't been to the movies for at least a month and as he's usually in and out of the New York repertory cinemas like a ferret, he, like me, doesn't worry about the age of the product. The last entertainment which we had witnessed together had been *An Evening with Josephine Baker*, so *The Prince of Thieves* would make a Nice Change.

We discovered later that the fortnightly film is usually an Indian one, which when dubbed into Greek is not all that easy to follow. Even the Greeks have difficulty (a) because the subtitles take up most of the screen and (b) they are cut so ruthlessly that the story line, if any, gets lost. But apparently they are bought by the yard, or the hour—as a great many Indian epics last anything up to six hours. Most simple audiences like them because of the exotic nature of the settings, and a great many of them are enormously spectacular and have huge casts of humans and animals.

68

The British or American films which reach the island are few and far between and are not dubbed. Instead they have Greek sub-titles, which are splendid for learning the language. Owing to the expense involved we never get any film less than a decade or so old. All the same, for the rest of the day we worked ourselves into a frenzy of anticipation over *The Prince of Thieves*.

The attraction was billed as commencing at 8.30 p.m. and foolishly we arrived a bit early. I say 'foolishly' because I have learned that when a time is mentioned, it is purely an approximation and there is no possibility of the film starting within an hour of the advertised time. Being well-brought-up I now treat the announcement like those lovely old-fashioned invites to dinner that used to read 'Seven o'clock for eight'.

There was a good deal of entertainment already going on in the place. It was swinging in Spiro's Café, which is the Hub of the Town even when it hasn't been turned into the Odeon once a fortnight. And as it's the post office, the telephone exchange and the village institute as well as a café, the coming and going is considerable. Sweets, cakes, yogurts, drinks are all sold there and endless games of cards and backgammon are embarked on.

This particular evening there was a plethora of very young children and very old gentlemen already seated in the auditorium. In front of them was a crumpled sheet which was to serve as a projection screen. Directly in front of it was a long greasy fly-catcher with thousands of victims which cast a giant shadow on the sheet. Below it sat a determined party of card players, thumping down their tricks in an abandoned way and, for all I know, continuing to do so after the show actually started at 9.10. Behind the bar, Spiro Theophrastus, the owner of the establishment, was doing a fabulous trade in soda-water, ouzo, orangeade and gazzoza (Greek fizzy-type lemonade). Rather sinister bits of fetta (goat's cheese) were being handed round on sticks; they smelt like mad and looked as if they had come hot feet from the goat in person.

Various members of the audience offered us some of this and indeed other refreshment and it was reassuring to realize that at

69

last we were no longer looked on by the village community as visitors from Outer Space. Gone, from this moment, were the days when the entire population followed us from shop to shop, pointing, speculating and giggling . . . It is true that neither Nelson nor I looked like visiting olive-pickers from a big town and we did appear to be the only non-Greek residents in the area, so it was quite an achievement to secure comparative anonymity. But from this night it was possible to relax and not endure that disconcerting and relentless staring which can be so demoralizing.

And inside the café there was a marvellously friendly atmosphere. For islanders with no television, few radios, no book or paper shops, the advent of the fortnightly cinema is an Event and there was not even any stamping at the delay. Perhaps they were reassured by the presence of the projectionist already at his post, tinkering with his machine in a haphazard but cheerful manner. It took up a good deal of space and was situated just in front of a window through which he kept hopping in and out, either (a) to pick up the bits that he had dropped on the way or (b) to pee. There was, I am bound to admit, not a great deal to inspire confidence in his actions and a reckless gaiety about his demeanour that gave an added excitement to the evening. Dmitri, the delightful son of Ho Pappas, was in charge of the box-office (walking) and kept shining his usherette's torch in the projectionist's face, which cannot have helped the latter much. Dmitri is obviously bound for greater things. He is the great Behind the Scenes authority and stage-manages the school graduation show, ties up and unties the ferry-boats, and performs various other social functions. Anyhow there he was taking our drachmae and climbing over the benches and chairs to do so. These are all borrowed from private houses and the school for every film festival but Spiro has told me I needn't bring mine all the way from To Spiti Mou.

Our chum, the portly policeman, arrived, beaming as usual, and started pinching sweets out of the show-cases and distributing them to all and sundry. He may have paid for them later but he is in fact the nearest thing to a criminal that I have seen yet on the island. There are three policemen and all are a bit prone to sweet-stealing. But all the financial negotiations in this part of the world have that fascinating Mediterranean casualness which is so attractive in this era of the down-payment. No one ever seems to pay for anything in our village AT THE TIME. This evening I tried in vain to settle for some cognac and ouzo consumed on Spiro's premises but I couldn't get him to take the money. 'Avrio, Kyrios Booool' (Tomorrow, Mr Bull) was his cry. No one else appeared to make any attempt to pay and I cannot believe he kept the orders in his head for longer than a few seconds.

Everyone was standing everybody else drinks which must have made it even more confusing. There was a great deal of moving of chairs and benches which meant that the whole seating plan got muddled. Knees were forced into bottoms or backs and the laughter got louder and louder. A lot of (to me) unfamiliar faces had clocked in, half obscured by those flat head-dusters that the ladies use to facilitate olive-basket carrying. During the season there is a big influx of outside workers from neighbouring islands or the mainland.

By nine o'clock the place was crammed and some people were practically the wrong side of the screen. Shortly afterwards the lights went out without warning and there was some frenzied torch-shining from the walking box-office. After a few seconds the lights went on again, long enough for the younger generation to start clambering over the seats to hit some of their friends before triumphantly returning to their seats. The din was tremendous and Spiro kindly put on his radio at full blast to even the effect.

The lights went out again and something was shown on the screen. For a few moments I thought I had either gone mad or blind or possibly both. The film looked like a surrealist nightmare, and it wasn't as if the fly-catcher was impeding our view still—in the short interval, in response to protests, Spiro Theophrastus had removed that. But the effect was quite extraordinary. The film was completely out of focus but even when some sort ot

picture emerged it did not remotely resemble any of the stills I had studied so assiduously in the morning. Then I got a clue. I saw a few Rolls-Royces. Now the R.R. is the only car that I ever recognize even in my native land. This failing threatens many of my relationships, through my omitting to notice that They have purchased a new vehicle. As I am usually sitting in it at the time it makes for a certain coldness. Anyhow there were all these R.R.s rolling around distributing ladies and gents in fancy-dress at churches and places. It took me quite a time to realize that it was a Royal wedding and even longer to place it as the one between Princess Irene of Greece and Don Juan, the Pretender, if that's the phrase, to the Spanish throne. It turned out to be a highly spectacular filmette, partic when in focus. It was followed by a musical short from Hungary in which muscular Magyar gents hammered away at their zithers while heavily moustached dittos did incredible things with their feet. It was all very enjoyable, the Lakka audience was spellbound and all running commentaries were temporarily suspended.

It finished all too soon and was followed by a seemingly interminable interval. During its course the projectionist dismantled the entire machine, smothered it with oil, hopped out of the window to pee yet again, hopped in again and landed on the head of an old man who woke with a start. Elsewhere there was much sweet-crunching and a bedlam-type noise but no one got up to stretch their legs, which was suprising as we were packed like sardines and cramp must have been rampant. We stood up in our seats so as not to spread alarm. There was enough of that going on in the immediate vicinity of the projector, which was looking very peculiar indeed, greasy and sulky. However, with a cynical shrug of his shoulders and a yell at Spiro to put the lights off, the projectionist gave it a sharp tap and we were off again.

This time we were off to the depths of Sherwood Forest in the County of Nottingham, England. And there were all our old friends, Messrs R. Hood, F. Tuck, L. John, etc. popping in and out of whizzing arrows, and Miss Maid Marian and the Lady

74

Christabel Something being rescued from incredible dangers. It was thick rich dramatic stuff and everything was made v. easy for Mr Hood and his M. Men because the guards (on the Other Side) were quite the silliest in the annals of historical film drama.

The Sound Projector, which was quite often so behind itself that it bore no relation to what was going on on the screen, was not a great help and I found occasionally that the Greek subtitles made more sense than the original English (well, American then) dialogue. But the whole thing was going down wonderfully with the audience, who were swallowing it hook, line and subtitle. Suddenly there was another interval while the reels were changed. At the risk of a double hernia N. and I got somehow to the door for a bit of fresh air. The atmosphere inside had become a bit unrarefied, to put it mildly and I suspect ungrammatically. There was no intermission bell but kind friends gave us plenty of warning to get back into our seats. The final phase of the drama of *The Prince of Thieves* was about to unfold in front of our very eyes, and all the loose ends were to be tied up—and there were quite a few of those I don't mind telling you. M. Marian and the Lady C. were stopped in the nick of time from being married to unsuitable bridegrooms and Mr Hood and his friend, Sir Alan, thinly disguised as one of the M. Men, took the girls, fresh from one altar to another, where F. Tuck took over and performed a fairly odd version of the Marriage Ceremony. It was an unconventional Solemnization of Holy M., and the words were hardly out of F. Tuck's mouth and on to the screen (by courtesy of the Sound Projector) a few seconds later, making them Husbands and Wives, when the Husbands were careering off on their chargers to help King Richard (about whom little had been said in the film up till then). King R. was apparently having a bit of a feud with King John, another royal personage who didn't get many days out of this film either. There was no hint of a Great Laundry Scene in the script that I heard.

But apparently the Right Side won and the entertainment ended as abruptly as it had begun. One couldn't help feeling that the poor ladies, who'd suffered so much during the evening to

get married, would have been better off wed to the villains of
the piece, who actually looked rather dears and did tend to stay
put a little longer than the heroes, who were never not off
swimming moats and/or climbing rope ladders to gain access to
unfriendly castles.

The audience was clearly satisfied however and there was quite
a bit of clapping at the end. We all exchanged our 'kallanick-
tasasses' (good nights) and Nelson and I wended our way up to
To Spiti Mou accompanied by fireflies and the sound of pounding
waves. We thought how nice it would be to arrive home and
find one of those jumbo period meals waiting for us, the sucking
pigs, swans and ducks piled high with veg, which seemed to
be standard table d'hôte fare for the Landed Gentry of those
days.

All we had was the remains of the Corned Beef Hash and a
glass of Koum Kwat, the bizarre liqueur they construct hereabouts out of midget sour oranges. And very nice too.

Owing to the preponderance of the afore-mentioned Indian
epics that came flickering across the Ionian screens I didn't get
around to visiting 'the local' again till two years later. Conditions
hadn't altered that much. Except that the stills hadn't arrived
from the capital and there was just a bleak announcement in ink
outside the butcher's (there was no meat that day) that a comedy
called *Lazybones* would be showing on the Friday. It was indeed
Friday and the usual equipment was already lodged inside Spiro's
Café. But Spiro himself told me that there was a hitch and something was wrong with the 'mekanika' (mechanics) and they would
not be ready till the Saturday. The fact was of course that the
projector was 'arostos' (ill) with the same malady that affects the
ferry-boat and the omnibus if their owners have subsequent more
attractive engagements which unfortunately prevent their presence
at a previous one.

As usual the film was announced as starting at 8 p.m. but in
spite of my house-guest's anxiety I insisted that arriving before
8.30 was lunacy, even if we did want to gawp at the celebrities

making an entrance. Actually only children were in their seats when we did get there and, after reassurances from Spiro that everything was 'endaxi' (O.K.), we started to wander through the town but didn't get further than Ho Raftis (the tailor). He is a dear gentle man who sells postcards, rugs and babies' potties, and re-does zips on the side, if you know what I mean.

Anyhow he insisted on offering us refreshment. As we had just swilled down a gargantuan meal with a great deal of Lefkimmi wine (from the south of Corfu) we didn't really want to indulge ourselves further. But it would have been churlish and certainly non-Greek to refuse. Sticky cakes were fetched from Spiro's Café and we sat round the sewing-machine, which has solved so many sartorial problems in downtown Lakka. Ho Raftis is a great optimist and has a vast stock of wares, some of which he has had in his shop for many years. An American friend of mine rather fancied an ornate rug he had on an upper shelf. It was slightly faded and shopworn and my chum thought he should have a reduction on the specified price. The tailor wouldn't budge (unlike most Mediterranean salesmen) and though Jimmy Mitchell visited him every day he stayed with me, in order to haggle, he was finally forced to buy it at what is called Starting Price in racing circles.

On the evening of the showing of *Lazybones* I was in the middle of the Great Canvas Shoe argument. I knew exactly what I wanted and Ho Raftis knew exactly what he wanted me to buy. His choice is some numbers he has in stock with white flaps on them. And I know that in Corfu you can get exactly the same white flapless. And these are what I desire. The shoes immediately available seem to me totally unmasculine and though I see various characters (male) prancing about the main drag in Lakka in them, they are not, I feel, for me. Truth to tell they are downright 'camp' and if I knew the Greek for this adjective I'd speak my mind to Ho Raftis.

No, on second thoughts I wouldn't as I don't want the word to reach Paxos for a very long time and by then it may have vanished from common parlance. And it will with any luck, as the whole conception of 'camp' is so changeable and transitory that vast areas of the world may with luck never be touched by the word or its essence. Personally I've never been able to define it properly myself. I certainly wasn't able to do so the other month when I happened to be in a New York nighterie called 'Downstairs and Upstairs', admiring for the umpteenth time the inimitable and eternal art of Miss Mabel Mercer. Although she has for a great many years been deemed perfectly capable of providing the only entertainment of the evening, on this occasion some lunatic had seen fit to precede her with another artiste. This was a saucy and not untalented young person who banged on far too long but had besprinkled her act with allusions to 'camp'.

During the interval, while awaiting the return of Miss Mercer, who would eventually emerge from the kitchen cum toilet area and ascend the podium with her usual dignity, a gent from the next table leaned over and said to me:

'We're from Texas. Could you please tell us what "camp" means?' And from the earnest expression on his face and that of his party I realized that he was not 'putting me on' (American for 'sending me up').

Well, it was quite a poser and I stammered and hummed and I think ha'ed and then passed. One of my companions, John Church the actor, considered the whole thing deeply. A man infinitely more articulate than I, and who indeed often assists me to put two words together, which you may have noticed is a feat I quite often have difficulty with, to say nothing of the grammatical problems or syntax dittos (what to do? I'm in the middle of one now. John Church where are you for heaven's sake?) anyhow eventually he (J.C.) surfaced, which I've just been able to do myself.

' "Camp",' said Mr Church as if sucking an imaginary pipe, 'is the whole area of saying, doing, wearing or even being extreme and often outrageous but just remaining this side of good taste.'

This explanation seemed to satisfy the Texans anyhow, but it is a phrase that has usually suffered from misinterpretation and over-use. A great many articles and treatises have been written about it and it's too late, and certainly quite out of place, for me to start analysing its importance on a literary level.

But for most people, like myself, the word has changed its meaning so much ever since one was first conscious of its use. And I'm not referring to 'camp' as put into juxtaposition with beds, stools and followers. I mean the use of the word as in the phrase 'Isn't he camp?' or 'He's a camp', which in my younger days meant that 'He' was a 'Pansy' or a 'Cissy', two other words that have totally confused and misled various bodies of people throughout the ages.

As at the time of writing this, an old Bette Davis or Joan Crawford film (or, come to think of it, a new one, partic if they are BOTH in it) is described as being 'madly camp', it is difficult to know where one is with the word.

I personally prefer words like 'Marmite' and 'Pudding' which never seem to change THEIR meaning. But of course one still gets shocks like when I found that Yorkshire Pudding was being served as 'Afters' in a Transport Café I frequent and being called 'Batter Pudding', because it had some Golden Syrup attached to it.

Anyhow you will be saying 'Now he HAS gone too far. What on earth have 'camp' or 'Yorkshire Pudd' got to do with a book purporting to be about Greece?'

And I do see your point. My goodness, things have come to a pretty pass, I do see that; but it has filled up a page and if you've got to write two hundred of them in order to put your mitts on a bit of moolah, you are jolly grateful for small mercies and diversions, like the sudden and totally unexpected appearance of the word 'camp'.

So where are we? Oh yes, on the way to see *Lazybones* at the Café—Post Office—Cinema. Well, the benches and chairs were placed at opposite ends of the room to where I remembered them on my last visit. In fact the projector was now stationed by the door, which must have made things a good deal easier for its master and avoided all that hopping in and out of the window.

Geoffrey Toone (the house guest at the time) and I sat near the machine so that we could have easy egress if the film proved too boring and/or incomprehensible. The audience trickled in and we exchanged the usual pleasantries and refreshments. Suddenly I saw the tall figure of Mr Ypsilos standing beside me and before I could stop him he'd plonked himself down and put his great be-carbuncled face into mine. My wicked landlord, whose flowing bowl has been filled by me rather than the other way round, always treats me as if he was an outsize moth fluttering round me, an outsize flame. The rest of the assembling audience were hugely delighted as any Ypsilos-Bull type situation is nectar to them, and they watched us avidly, waiting for poste or riposte, badinage, or a brisk exchange of blows. It was clear that they looked on us as a possible curtain-raiser to *Lazybones*. I played up to all this as outrageously as usual and pointed out to Mr Ypsilos with copious gestures that his head would block the lens of the projector. I tried to intimate to him that this portion of his anatomy could not really compare with the scheduled film as satisfactory entertainment. I didn't even bring his carbunclage into it. He remained unconvinced and glued to his seat, fascinated (a) by the possibility of the distinguished-looking Mr Toone being a millionaire and (b) by my involvement in Greek and English with the projectionist's assistant, who had seen me recently in a film in Athens and this sort of thing spelled danger. You see, up till last year I had been trying to pose to the islanders as an impoverished but hard-working writer. This suited me admirably as I was treated like an eccentric recluse. I think I rightly assumed that a member of the literary profession was liable to be more respected and considered more respectable and certainly less wealthy than an actor.

It is a curious thing that in the layman's eyes anyone remotely connected with the film industry must automatically have two sports cars, a sex life of extraordinary variety and a swimming-pool in the *sitz-platz*. But, gentle reader, it isn't true and I know that if I'd told the projectionist's assistant what I really earned in the film he'd just seen (*Licensed to Kill* produced by Puck films from a bed-sit off the Edgware Road) he would have fallen through the lens. But this last year the cat was well and truly out of the bag because not only had *Doctor Strangelove* been showing in Corfu but some Paxiot's aunt had caught me on the Merv Griffin TV show while she was staying with relatives in Detroit. As a result of these two catastrophes I had to abandon the pretence that 'Oh, yes, there IS an actor exactly like me. Yes, I know the one you mean. I'm always being mistaken for him', that I have kept up so long and valiantly. I had even suggested that they might be confusing me with Mr Robert Morley or Miss Tessie O'Shea but now I had to face the music and the projectionist's assistant was not likely to ease matters.

The sad thing is that they don't expect much of me. They don't expect me to build a theatre or a cinema or even a Palace of Fun, which is what Miss Joan Littlewood is fully prepared to do. No, all they want is to see one of my films. At least that's what it seems they want. It is possible that they cannot believe that I'm an actor, as apart from my bizarre appearance I don't think there is much else to indicate that I tread the boards. But, they say, why can't I ask somebody to send one of my films for showing in Paxos. I have tried to point out that even the hiring of *Doctor Strangelove* for one night would cost a fortune. And even if I was Mr C. Chaplin or Miss E. Taylor I would question the wisdom, quite apart from the extravagance, of having all one's old films sent over. Actually I think I would pay for some of them NOT to be shown on the island. The ghastly thing is it is just conceivable that one or two of the numbers I was in just before or just after the war might turn up. What a horrifying thought! Supposing they got hold of *The Silent Voice* (so silent that it was only to be caught in the Tott Court Road one Sunday) or *Hammer the Toff*. Oh lawks! I would have to leave the island until things blew over. Well, let's leave that one until it surfaces. In the meantime I have tried to point out to the interested parties that, because one has appeared in a film, it is not 100 per cent certain that one can control its destination or indeed destiny and, until all interest has evaporated in it as a property, the producers hang on to the copies like kangaroos with their babies.

So I tried to convey this to the projectionist's assistant who should have known about these things but Mr Ypsilos was riveted by it all and kept on cross-questioning the P.A. about getting hold of a film of mine. As usual I played dumb and just glared at him if he spoke to me.

It was now well past nine and the projectionist indicated to all and sundry that he was ready to start. Spiro removed his lamp from the centre of the ceiling, and then the overloaded fly-catcher. A few hundred yards of blank film were run off. At least they were blank until a perfect reproduction of Mr Ypsilos's head was reproduced, complete with carbuncle. A great deal of yelling and shouting ensued, at the end of which he was forcibly removed to the side, chair and all, protesting the while. I seized the moment to play to the public by making shadow pictures on the screen. Mr Toone, who was better at it than I, had what they call in press quotes 'a big personal success' with his mimes of rabbits and mice. I did simple things like hitting or pretending to shoot myself.

Anyhow we got a great number of laughs and the audience was in high fettle at the slight discomfiture of Mr Ypsilos. He just sat staring at Geoffrey, willing him to make a bid for his land. The film was now really ready to start and Spiro put out the last light in the building. Usually he manages to leave this one burning (it's in the kitchen) because he likes to keep dishing out the ouzo and coffee during the show. But owing to pressure from all sides he had to decide whether to watch the film, or serve the customers as on previous occasions. The film won and we were in complete darkness. I only hope he got more out of it than we did. *Lazybones* turned out to be a wildly overacted Greek comedy in which everyone went eight million times too far. Grimaces and quadruple takes were being dished out with monotonous regularity by the entire cast. The action appeared to take place in a perfume factory and I don't mind telling you that the whole thing stank to highest heaven. Just before the first intermission we slunk out from boredom, carefully creeping under the lens to avoid having our exit register on the screen.

Also to avoid Mr Ypsilos, currently in zizz-land and snoring away ever so happily.

The next film we were promised was *The Sands of Iwo Jima* with John Wayne, which should be better than nothing as it will have the original sound track. Whether we shall actually hear anything will depend on what animal or human is tampering with the generator which is left outside the building to supply the juice for everything.

Although the Greek comedies I have seen are anathema to me, the serious films are sometimes of very high calibre indeed. In spite of the comparatively recent emergence of the film industry in Greece great strides have been made and some of the direction and photography is sensationally original. There appears to be very little censorship and the freedom has led to some remarkable films. I saw a psychotic thriller in Corfu recently which contained a rape or two, some nude bathing and several sequences which would never have got away with it in swinging Wardour Street. But there seemed to be no H or indeed A certificate and the kiddiwinks were having a ball.

The day after the première (and last night) of *Lazybones* I saw the projectionist and apologized for our seeming rudeness. He also thought it an indifferent film. But he told us about John Wayne.

'You'll love that,' he said. And I expect we will. And so will the whole village. Isn't it marvellous to be living somewhere where there are no reviews and 'Going to the Movies' is in itself a major social occasion?

6. *The Three Ferry-Boats*

Apart possibly from the film industry, a sense of competition appears to rule the trading situation in Greece even more than elsewhere; it is not unusual to find about twelve bootshops next door to each other, and in our village of Lakka there are many grocers all offering the same tins of corned beef, bottles of ouzo and packets of envelopes. An identical situation has spread to the steamship department plying between Corfu and Paxos.

Though the demand is as yet mild, to put it mildly, we have a plethora of machines transporting us back and forth. They are a mixed bag of vessels. The smartest, I suppose, is the *Epta Nissos* (Seven Islands), which not only has a first-class section, where I've never seen anyone except those who have been taken queer during the passage, but also a superstructure where one can sit down and look at the scenery. The Greeks usually stay huddled in the cabin as they seem to dread the open air and sun and would prefer to have a good zizz. I and other strangers (or comparatively) love being up top and there is not as much danger as there used to be of being asphyxiated by the gaseous fumes proceeding from the engine-room. This is because the funnel, which was poised perilously here till recently, fell off last year into the sea just opposite my house. They haven't replaced it and no one seems to have noticed its absence except me. The *Epta Nissos* is the most punctual, the fastest and most reliable of the fleet. She is usually captained by Marco, a young, short man with a dazzling smile. His father sometimes takes over, particularly early in the season, to keep his hand in.

But my favourite ferry-boat is the *Ephstasia*, which is known by most people as 'The Pullman' because her cabin is seated rather like a train carriage's. She possesses an inside loo of great beauty (it even provides seating accommodation) and an enchanting captain called Mitsos (short for Dmitri, they tell me) who gives me Greek lessons on the voyage and ticks me off severely when I make errors. His English is sketchy in the extreme and I still find it disconcerting to be bidden 'Bye-Bye' the moment I see him. But this is a common occurrence with Greeks and what else could one expect from a nation who say 'nay' (yes) with a shake of the head, and 'okki' (no) with a nod of the ditto, and whose usual method of saying farewell is to beckon with their hands. The captain of The Pullman says 'Never mind. Never mind.' a good deal, which is very comforting when in deep conversational trouble.

Mitsos is warm and over-generous like most seafaring men. Nothing is too much trouble for him to get me in Corfu and on the voyage over I am always invited to share his luncheon. The third mate (aged about twelve) prepares this, which is usually composed of hard-boiled eggs, home-made olive oil, extremely smelly but nutritious fetta and marvellously fresh bread, which I suspect has been baked by his pretty wife. The Mitsoses live in Lakka and it is seemingly impossible to return their kindness, though I try to augment the cross-channel meals with some uninsulting luxuries like sweet biscuits, fruit, or those delightfully honey-soaked pastries, which are so obviously slimming.

The third ship of the line is the good ship *Aspasia*, which has a fruity Rabelaisian skipper with a superb knowledge of seamanship. I sometimes think she is the most seaworthy of the three and I have been in her in some rough seas I don't mind telling you. Her captain has friends who entertain him in every port (some of the waits in harbour are interminable) and a very near-sighted son called Vassilys who acts as chief engineer and first mate. Throughout the voyage father and son scream at each other from one end of the boat to the other, but they are both great dears and, as with the other boats, will not accept a drachma from me when I journey from Lakka to Gaios. The number of free trips my friends and I have had are legion. The skipper lives in Loggos, our half-way stop, and usually pops off there and lets his son take over while he slips her from the jetty and potters off home.

How the ships make money I wouldn't know. I recently brought over just the twelve large packages on The Pullman and was not asked to pay a lepta (a hundred go to a drachma) for them. The fare across is only thirty-five drachmae (about eight shillings) for a three and a half hour trip, five hours if you go on to Gaios. My luggage on this occasion included a refrigerator, a bed and a mattress, none of which are exactly stowable pieces. It doesn't affect this issue that there was a vital piece missing from the fridge when I got it home.

But to get back to the ferry-boats. In the off-season months the clientèle is mainly composed of battered old islanders and those curious ladies who seem totally unmoved by rough seas, funnels falling off and other hazards of the voyage and just settle themselves in an odd corner and resemble nothing so much as bundles of clothes assembled at the last moment for a jumble sale. Sometimes goats, sheep, horses, cows and indeed children are hoisted on board and left secured to some bastion for the duration of the trip.

In the summer the Sunday Joint for the village arrives live and kicking of a Friday, and the moment it sees land, the poor thing, it tends to make a wild dash for the open country, only to find most of the population waiting to drive it to the grazing-ground to enable it to have a last tuck-in. It will stay happy for a bit longer, little knowing that it is chewing within a few yards of the abattoir which will constitute its last resting-place on this earth, always excepting our stomachs.

During the season the morale of the ships' companies is hoisted by the physical and sartorial change in their customers. Casual tourists will be joined by vibrant and indubitably sexy young persons, some of whom are bound for the skin-diving establishment run by the Club Méditerranée in Gaios. They lie about the boats in extraordinary positions with very little on, watched, with only faint interest seemingly, by the local passengers, swathed up to the neck in woollies and black shawls. Yet for the most part a unique *bonhomie* exists between the passengers and crews of these ships and as long as the weather and seas are pleasant every trip is like a picnic. Meals are shared, bottles of wine are handed around and everyone has a ball. The number of people who get their hands on the wheel during the voyage is legion. This is not suprising as Paxos is an island of seamen and ex-seamen. The personal relationship between the native salts is oddly moving and in so many of them, as you watch them at the helm, you can see that desire to possess a ship of their own.

The length of stay of the ships at ports varies with the different captains, their capacity or desire for refreshment and how many friends or relations they have in the immediate vicinity of the harbour. An additional complication in the Paxos harbours is that sometimes before berthing, the younger passengers just strip off and dive into the crystal-clear water. This impedes manoeuvring and involves a great deal of shouting and abuse and difficulty in getting the truants back on board. Yet one feels the captains would never leave anyone behind and they certainly never refuse any reasonable request to deliver something. If I have urgent mail I give it to one of the captains and can be sure of it being posted in Corfu that afternoon, thus saving the day I would lose by handing it to Spiro Café, whose hands are tied, figuratively speaking. If it is sent through him, he keeps it in the cash, string and mail drawer near the sweets until a bus is going to Gaios.

Anyhow, short of carrier pigeons, which is quite a serious idea of the illustrator of this book and myself, the ferry-boat is the quickest and most reliable form of communication. It is also very easy to time things as the boats pass under my terrace and there is plenty of warning owing to the hooting that goes on. In fact hardly a morning goes by without appalling exhibitions in reply from me. I have run out of innovations and the performances now incline to monotony. I present arms with a broom, wearing a basin on my head, to The Pullman; cut out the basin bit for the *Epta Nissos*; and just wave and jump about at the *Aspasia* because her crew are always busy sorting out the fantastic cargo which she specializes in, and are therefore disinclined for droll by-play. But it has become quite a ritual and newcomers to the island arriving by sea are plainly flabbergasted by the behaviour of the eccentric Kyrios in the 'aspro spiti' (white house). I say it's a daily occurrence but that's not exactly true. Though the craft vary in seaworthiness it has to be very inclement for a voyage to be cancelled for that reason. A holiday or a misunderstanding with one of the other ships is far more likely a cause and it is bewildering how often, when I want to go to Corfu for a particular reason, the ferry-boat fails to turn up.

Quite often there is no warning at all and the other day I was standing fairly spick-and-span, with my luggage packed, when Alekkos came up the hill to tell me that there was no boat that day. 'Why not?' I asked, and was told that it was 'arostos' (literal translation, 'ill'). This, I have learned to my cost, is the usual excuse given for any failure in public transport. Furiously I unpacked and sat on the terrace, typing and sulking alternately. Shortly afterwards I heard violent hooting and The Pullman came whizzing by crammed with children screaming 'Kyrios Bull' at the tops of their voices. Apparently it was a school holiday and Mitsos had decided to take the children on a round the island picnic.

'Never mind,' said Alekkos who gave me the info, 'children happy. You go Corfu tomorrow. Never mind!' And of course on this occasion, apart from irritation, there was no damage done and the children were happy indeed.

But sometimes an emergency combined with this seeming irresponsibility can create an alarming situation, though I must confess that, as long as the weather is not appalling, some odd caïque is always popping over even if she is only bound for the south of the island and not the capital. I remember one crisis being averted by just such a thing happening. N. had had some disquieting news from home and thought it advisable to fly back to Atlanta immediately. But we were in Corfu at the time and had to go to Paxos to pick up his effects. We caught the *Aspasia*, which was looking more like a floating laundry than usual; short-sighted Vassilys had apparently hoisted some of his wardrobe to the masthead so that his father couldn't see properly from the steering position and kept on yelling at him.

N. retired to the roof of the ship to get some final sun, a position I cannot attain for fear of toppling over the side into the thalassa. We knew we should have to return to Corfu the following day in order to catch the plane to Athens on which we were booked and it was with horror that I learned from Vassilys that neither he, his father, nor the fairly good ship *Aspasia* had the slightest intention of moving out of Loggos Harbour for several days. That is where the vessel berthed as the Captain lives there. We had passed the *Epta Nissos* in mid-ocean so to speak and I knew for a fact that The Pullman was in dry dock undergoing repairs and for once was genuinely 'arostos' (ill).

So that disposed of all three ships, movement-wise, and things looked a bit hopeless. We were up the creek not only without a paddle but without a paddle-steamer. I sat on a case of gazzoza (fizzy lemonade) and wondered how to break the news to N. and whether it would make him lose his balance. Suddenly a young gent approached from nowhere and asked if I was English. I said I thought I was and he told me that he spoke the English very good. So I said yes indeed he did and what was he going to

Paxos for? Did he live there for instance? Oh no, he said, emphatically, with that slight sneer all Corfiotes have when discussing the beautiful island on which I live from time to time. He added that he was off there to search for some 'astikoses' (pretend lobsters that are very much in demand and not all that plentiful; they are large crayfish without any claws and don't blush so much when popped into boiling water). He was apparently going to take them back to his restaurant in Cavos, at the southern tip of Corfu, where the ferry-boat stops on each voyage. He looked every bit of sixteen, which seemed a trifle young for a restaurateur, but I've been rapidly learning to be surprised by nothing that happens in Greece, partic when it emanates from the young.

My ears came out like stalks at his disclosures. Cautiously I asked him how he was intending to get the beasts back to Corfu. Being only too fully conscious of the fallibility of transport between the islands, I had a curious fantasy of him swimming across in a great aquarium with an outboard motor. He said he was coming back the next day. 'The next day,' I said, and he told me that his uncle would be taking the lobsters and him in his caïque. I informed him of our dilemma and he disarmingly said oh, but of course we must go with his uncle who'd be honoured, etc. I reported the outcome of this conversation to N., who looked a bit sceptical but brightened considerably when I asked him to consider the possibility of a lobster-type lunch thrown in. We both felt our mouths watering a tidge at the thought. Accordingly we were on the jetty early and found the usual collection of goats, pigs and refugees or what looked like refugees.

'Uncle had better have a pretty big caïque,' observed N.

It was 9.30 but it was at least an hour later when 'The Lobster Special' arrived. Our nerves were a bit frayed by that time and we were thinking of pinching the nearest dinghy and rowing for it. But we all piled into the caïque and prepared for a not wildly luxurious journey. The youthful restaurant proprietor had assured me that there was a bus from his establishment and we could easily catch it after a long and comfortable lunch. I realized that he realized he had two extra big fish in his net, and he might just as well have put us into the vast crate, stuffed with shell-fish and seaweed. There was never any doubt as to what we were having for our midday meal, it was just a question of which. We stationed ourselves very near the dear things and watched the restaurateur opening the lid, prior to dousing them almost affectionately with sea-water which he brought up over the side in a bucket. N. and I assisted him generously, drooling a bit and thinking how super it was going to be around oneish.

The astikoses were still nipping a bit and it was impossible to put a 'reserved' or 'sold' sign on the ones we had selected in what can only be described as our minds' eyes. But there was no demand from the other passengers and no one seemed remotely interested in the crate and its contents *per se*, though the younger goats were alarmed by the amount of water which was being sloshed down the side of the ship from time to time. It was also affecting the rear portions of what appeared at first sight to be large bundles of clothing but turned out on closer inspection to be, as usual, old ladies. They sat there in the damp, gesticulating and shaking their fists at the young restaurant proprietor but every now and then breaking into toothless and maniacal laughter.

In order to keep a watchful eye on the lunch N. and I had to sit right over the engine and the vibration was terrifying. Eventually, after a far from smooth voyage, we arrived at the sandy beaches of Cavos. The Lobster Special drew too much water to get alongside the jetty but a small boat came out, driven by a sort of cheerful Charon. Goodness I've just looked up Charon in the *Classical Dictionary of Proper Names*, which natch I always have at hand, and I can't resist reading you and you reading the riveting details of the son of Erebos and Nox, who conducted the souls of the dead across the rivers Styx and Acheron. He was imprisoned for a year because he ferried Hercules without the golden bough which served as a passport. Charon is represented as an old man, robust but with a hideous countenance, long white beard and piercing eyes. It was usual among the ancients to place money under the tongue of the deceased to pay the boatman's fare. But as many of the customers, if they hadn't had a proper funeral, weren't allowed to take passage without previously wandering on the shore for a hundred years, it is v. likely that the fares might have gone up by the time they actually got on board.

Anyhow, the boatman, come to think of it, has not the slightest resemblance to Charon, apart from the robust countenance, but the story has filled up a bit of a page and it might help the compositors of this book. Did you know how tricky it is to get the drawing actually to face the page to which it refers? This, owing to binding difficulties, may become apparent in this tome of mine so please excuse me if I drool on more than usual from time to time. But we were transported to the jetty by this man, who on investigation does not resemble Charon remotely, along with three goats, a gigantic sewing-machine with treadles, and six passengers. By the time we were all in the small boat, the waterline was only just above the sea and a false step might have qualified us for a trip with Charon himself (Oh, gosh I wish we could get rid of him!), but eventually we made the jetty. We followed the lobsters, selected the largest when the crate finally came to rest in the garden of the restaurant, and pottered off for a bathe before lunch.

We had a magical time in the sea (it is one of the best beaches in Corfu) and subsequently a miraculous meal. We didn't begin to feel sentimental over the huge boiled thing with claws which was brought to the table, though we had followed its career so closely. I had wondered what would happen to the rest of the proprietor's haul, as his establishment was too remote to dispose of them all, but my query was answered as we went to our table. Several high-powered speedboats had clocked in, captained by a lot of high-powered young men in gay hats, who had heard (doubtless by Lobster Post) what was for cooking. They were all managers of hotels and restaurants in and around Corfu who were able to charge the earth for the delicacy. It is an extraordinary fact that lobster all over the world is seemingly the same phenomenal price, whether you are in London, Paris, New York or Cavos.

I don't know what these young gents paid for the fish retail but I know that our lunch cost about the equivalent of a week's stay at a reasonable hotel. Mark you, it was worth it, as indeed anything is if you happen to want a certain commodity at a certain time, but it is curious that lobsters appear to cost as much whether they are plentiful or not.

We were sitting under a white mulberry tree. I had never seen one before. N. looked up and one of the fruit fell straight into his mouth which was fortunately open. He swallowed twice and reported that it was delicious. I looked up, opened my mouth, and nothing fell at all. The tree was too high to shake from where we were. A cool wine from Lefkimmi had washed the lobsters down beautifully and we were very content. I asked the proprietor what we could have for 'afters'. He pointed above our heads and in a moment a tiny child went scaling up the tree with a basket, closely followed by N., who likes that sort of thing anyhow. They descended with a mass of the delicious fruit and we had another bottle of wine. Half an hour later, in the middle of a sun-drenched coma, I realized there was no sign of a bus. I summoned the patron. He said he was sorry but it was Saturday. I asked him what the hell that had to do with it and he said on Saturdays the bus started from Lefkimmi some miles away. Where the wine comes from I said. Where the wine comes from he agreed. I began to get a bit panicky and tetchy. The young gentleman said 'Never Mind', it would be quite all right. His father would drive us there as he had to go with the remaining lobsters.

We relaxed and finished the wine. Suddenly we heard an engine revving up, but instead of a lorry or at worst a jeep heaving into view it was a motorized bicycle with a small trailer which just about held the crate which we had come to know so intimately. N. and I sat on this and were bumped about almost silly as the vehicle made slow progress along a primitive road. The proprietor's father who actually and naturally turned out to be the proprietor himself (and not, I suppose, necessarily even the young gentleman's father) dropped us off at a café where many merry gents were singing. A hitherto unknown traveller assured us that the bus would stop there and gave us a turcico coffee. A few minutes later a very classy bus drove up and took us on board. An hour and a half later we were safely in the capital city.

All's well that ends well and I'm bound to say I have mostly been very fortunate when seemingly stuck on Paxos. Apart from stray trading caïques there is an erratic service to Lefkimmi, the industrial capital of the island. This can be a ravishing voyage because half an hour after passing Cavos, one finds oneself gliding up a very narrow river. It requires quite exceptional seamanship and it always reminds me of the colossal hash I made during the war going up and down the Beaulieu river. No ship in the history of landing-craft has ever touched bottom with its flat ditto more often than mine.

The water up to Lefkimmi is very shallow indeed and there is no room for a fair-sized caïque to turn safely, so most of them have to come down stern first. But many craft use the tiny port and the portion of the town where one berths is extremely attractive. There is a small bridge and a café run by a lady called Antigone after that lady (am at the Classical Dictionary again!) who buried her brother against the king's orders and found herself condemned to be buried alive for her pains. But she killed herself before they got at her and the king's son committed suicide on her grave. Not a frightfully cheerful family but it must be remembered that she was dear old Oedipus's daughter which might account for things not going quite right.

Anyhow the Lefkimmi Antigone kindly gives us plates and cutlery from which we eat the picnic lunch, washed down by her wine. If the wait for the three o'clock bus is a long one it is expedient to go and lie in the olive groves by the river, which are smashingly cool. Otherwise it tends to be very tiring being the Entertainment for the day supplied to the Local Inhabs who at this time of day seem to have fewer resources in themselves than folk from other areas. In Lefkimmi they come out in droves and stare at one in a disconcerting fashion.

The bus journey to Corfu is less boring than the same one by sea.

As long as not too many of the passengers are being sick into the paper bags kindly supplied by the transport authorities, it can be an interesting drive and one glimpses some of the more improbable parts of the island, like the sand dunes of Korissia which fringe the lagoon. One also passes the bungalow hotel at Miramare beach, where far more English is spoken than at the Regent Palace, London.

But, though this mode of travel makes a nice change, I like the atmosphere on the ferry-boats far more and am quite content to spend the extra time in actual travel, and it has to be very urgent business in Corfu which prevents me waiting for a genuine ferry-boat. I have a great admiration for them and their crews; and their courage and tenacity in what must essentially be a very routine job are remarkable. I have seen them put to sea in fearsome gales and not long ago the third or fourth mate of one of the craft was swept overboard without anyone noticing his absence until they reached harbour. As a result of this tragedy planks of wood have been added to the gunwales to lessen the chances of it occurring again but I doubt if they will prove infallible.

Incidentally there is a strange attitude to death in these parts which at first sight appears callous and astringent. Yet I suppose, for a race who Enjoy life with a capital E so much and do so little apparent grizzling and grumbling through it, it seems quite natural to eat, drink and be what looks like Merry at funerals. All those I've attended in villages in Greece have been far gayer than the weddings. And the food and drink, usually served outside the church, have been high quality stuff.

Perhaps they don't fear death or old age as much as the more supposedly advanced nations. It seems to me that in Greece everyone is enchanting to their old relations and there is never any question of them being neglected or abandoned. The children are courteous to them and hardly hit them at all. It must be confessed however that they hit each other a good deal but it is all in fun. Some of the horseplay indulged in by the older gents in my village is astonishing and very moving. Family ties are as strong as they are in all the Mediterranean Catholic countries and nowhere can this be more clearly seen than in the three ferry-boats plying between Paxos and Corfu.

Two of the ships have a father-son, captain-first mate relation-ship usually in operation and one of them had two sons as crew until the younger was abstracted for military service. This family tie-up really does seem to work and both the *Epta Nissos* and the *Aspasia* sail smoothly enough, in spite of the occasional yelling match on the latter. The third father just comes down to the jetty whenever The Pullman is due to slip and wishes her luck. Every now and then he explains to passengers:

'I am the father of Mitsos, the Captain.'

And knowing his son, I don't mind telling you that it's not a bad thing to be.

7. Sir, Your Post Office Has Been Struck by Lightning

Quite a few of us are familiar with the now legendary phrase which appeared in an old *Traveller's Language Guide*: 'Sir, the Postilion has been struck by lightning.'

When I first heard about it I have to admit that I came to the conclusion that opportunities to use it seemed strictly limited, but only the other day I longed for a Greek phrase book which might have been able to help me in slightly similar circumstances. But it was the post office which had been struck by lightning and I did happen to be in it at the time. How tremendously effective and moving it would have been and how good for British prestige abroad if I had been able to turn to the Postmaster-General of Paxos and announce to him in a cool but definitely reassuring voice: 'Sir, your Post Office has been struck by lightning.'

Mark you, he mightn't have been in the least impressed;

98

it's conceivable that his post office is always being struck by lightning. And this particular instance would have been considered small fry, being a tiny strike or strikette and only catching the iron part of the window fastenings. But it did make a jolly good crackling sound which was unmistakable. In my American-born *Say It In Greek* there are no allowances for this particular type of disaster and phrases like 'Where IS the American consul?' and 'Can YOU help me jack up the car?' weren't going to get us anywhere in this situation. The unfortunate occurrence also made it extremely difficult for me to have the row with the P.M.G., which I'd been rehearsing from my village to Gaios. But, if a chap's habitat has been struck by lightning, it doesn't seem quite cricket to strike while the iron is hotter than usual, if you know what I mean. I'm sure I don't.

Nelson and I had decided to pay a personal visit to see why mail from America, which at absolute best could reach Corfu in three or four days, then took an additional four days to get to us. Not only was there this delay but in those days one had to sign for mail. This was apparently because Greeks who live in America are constantly sending dollars back and the authorities want to make certain that any enclosures have not been nicked before arrival. As nobody ever sends me money from America (indeed it is usually the reverse way round) it had got me mad; the situation was even worse for poor N., who was anxiously awaiting news from Atlanta, Georgia, where his Mum was poorly. An additional complication was the fact that the postman wanted one to sign in person as it were. I have now come to an arrangement by which Spiro Café or Alekkos do this for me but in those days it turned out that if one wasn't on hand for one of the postman's tri-weekly visits, the letters from America just went back to the capital until his next jaunt.

Ordinary letters tend to come on the last bus of the day which arrives long after I have ascended the hill to cope with dinner or have a nice game of Scrabble. It must be admitted that the postman will actually pay us a visit if there is a telegram or registered letter to deliver (and stops to enjoy a few digestive biscuits). I try to reason with him about the mail situation but he is unable to explain its manifold frustrations. Lakka gets the thinnest end of the wedge as great sacks of the stuff arrive in the ferry-boat every afternoon and are carted off to Gaios to be distributed from there. Sometimes, if I'm expecting something really important, I trek into the capital on the off chance. And that is exactly why N. and I were there on the fatal afternoon. We had hardly put our feet inside the building before the damned thing was struck, which made my position as regards the Post-master-General equivocal (I think that's the word I mean; it'll have to do anyhow). After all, his home from home had narrowly escaped disaster. I must point out that Gaios Post Office is on the first floor of a private house and, as there is no sign outside the door, a great many people never find it. It is also up a side street away from the town centre.

Looking back on the Incident I think that the P.M.G. cannot have been quite himself that particular afternoon, lightning or no lightning. He had his mac on even before it struck, as if aware of impending disaster, like Cassandra—not that she wore a mac. Anyhow, visibly shaken by the whole thing, he blenched a bit when I popped my head through the hole in the wall. I decided not to Raise Hell and instead handed him a large envelope containing business documents and asked how much by air to England please (parra kalor). He got out the largest piece of paper conceivable and after ten minutes intense concentration and covering the paper with figures he announced that it would cost thirty-seven drachmae and twenty lepta. During this performance a large proportion of the population of Gaios had come up the stairs to see how the P.M.G. had survived the afternoon. The place was abuzz. All sorts of characters put their heads through the hole, and when I finally got mine in again I said I thought the price excessive and asked him how much by sea (thalassa), pointing at it. It looked at that moment an extremely hazardous form of transport. He laughed like a maniac and retreated back to his piece of paper, which he reversed. By the time he had reached his next conclusion the post office was seething and at least ten per cent had genuine business to transact. So when he told me that it would cost nineteen drachmae (five shillings) to send my package by thalassa I settled for it, as I was getting a bit nervous about the people of Gaios, who obviously thought that Friday was a good day for playing post office, especially when there was hope of a thunderstorm or three.

We left reluctantly because we could see a huge sack of mail sitting on the floor by the P.M.G.'s feet and which indeed could be struck by lightning at any minute. We had followed its progress throughout the afternoon, from the moment we boarded the fairly good ship *Aspasia* at Lakka and saw it in the hold. We had disembarked with it and some of it would join us on The Two Brothers, the omnibus (To Leoforio), when we went home. This machine is a highly individual vehicle. It has its name on the front, as does one of the island's lorries. They are driven by, guess what, two brothers. They are very sweet gents and the driver of the bus never leaves Gaios without rounding up tardy customers in bars and giving a great many toots on his horn.

Although the journey from the capital to Lakka need only take twenty minutes it very rarely does it in that time. For the two brothers' mother lives half-way along the route and what the hell's the use of owning your own bus if you can't stop when and for as long as you like? It's not as if there was any competition. Sometimes the driver gathers his wife up there. On St Constantine's Day The Two Brothers was bedecked with flowers and flags; we stopped at the house and my chum and I, the only passengers that day, were invited in to ouzo and pasta. There was quite a party going on and Michaelis, the driver, played us some Beatle records to make us feel at home. After about an hour we resumed our journey. In front of the family residence there is a Bus Cemetery where we stop and pay a silent tribute. They are machines which were driven by Michaelis's father and grand-father. They lie peacefully a few steps from the front door and I swear I saw a wreath on the roof of one once.

On the evening of the storm The Two Brothers took longer than usual on her journey. She stopped continually and went careering up cart-tracks at whim, where she collected sacks of olives from outlying farms. As they would have to be delivered at the olive press and the bus was already running an hour late, N. and I decided to get out and walk some way from Lakka. There was no question of our getting at the mail, though it was lying in the bus some feet from us, quiet as a mouse.

An infuriating situation and in a way perhaps it would have been less maddening if the Postmaster-General had announced to us earlier with saturnine Greek glee:

'Sirs, your mail has been struck by lightning.'

8. *Loneliness of the Short-Distance Writer*

My friends constantly express surprise that anyone as gregarious as I can be content to spend such lengths of time on a remote Greek island. 'Anyhow,' they say, 'you loathe the country.'

It isn't true, the accusation I mean. What I don't like is spending nights in foreign beds, and I don't mean what you mean or think I mean, you filthy beasts. What I don't like is all that travelling back and forth over short distances and spending sleepless nights in beautiful comfortable beds but ones to which I'm not used.

The fact is that I'm not a week-ender by nature. Not having regular employment, Saturday and Sunday don't seem particularly special to me, though I do notice that there are a lot more fresh, attractive, witty people around at that period, and they do seem more plentiful and, I fear, wickeder in the metropolitan area than in the highways and byways. Anyhow it is definitely quieter in London of a Sunday and I simply don't believe it when chums from the country ring up and say how lovely and relaxing it is down there. So peaceful, they add. I think it's a downright lie in most cases. From cock-crow (and boy does it crow) until sunset the air is rent by noise, and things like gates closing or bells ringing tend to sound like H-bombs going off by mistake in the upstairs loo. And everyone sings. Goodness how they sing! It all makes me very edgy and gritty.

But then I am about as ungracious a guest as you could have. I cannot pretend that I'm all that gracious a host but at any rate in that case it is more O.K. to bite the hand that feeds me.

I have to admit that the moment I enter someone else's building knowing that I'm a guest there for a period I feel as if I were being imprisoned or, worse, back at school. I've now reached the age where I rarely sleep properly unless I am in my own bed with My Things around me. It seems a bit affected to cart them all down into the country for a night or two. My Things, it must be pointed out, include a great many animals (no, not live), favourite books and a few hundred photographs. Having no motor car (I've never learned to drive properly) I am usually forced to take public transport. Country people rarely use this mode of conveyance and tend to dismiss any problem airily with silky phrases like, 'My dear, it COULDN'T be easier. We're only forty minutes away and ALL the trains are non-stop. Yes the 11.20 is a SUPER train.' If one is travelling on a Sunday, partic in summer-time, trains behave far from normally. Lines are being worked on, certain stations are closed and the whole expedition becomes like one of those jaunts organized by Hillary and Hunt (and how I've longed for a Sherpa when caught in a muddle at Ealing Broadway).

I remember vividly being invited for lunch at Denham, Bucks. 'Only an hour door to door,' said my dear hosts cheerfully on the blower; and my friend and I arrived at Marylebone station one Sunday morning. It's a terminus I'm quite fond of in a desultory way and I was busy writing out rude things on the lettering machine when we were informed by loudspeaker that actually no trains were leaving that particular station that morning. They did however invite us to take a bus to Wembley which would connect with a station which was operating. Wembley, I ask you! We had first-class tickets too, which we'd bought a few minutes before from an obviously very ill-informed box-office man. They didn't seem to carry much weight on the omnibus when we tried to sit with the driver. At Wembley there was a delayette or bijou delay and we finally had a very nice lunch at downtown Denham with our friends at the continental hour of three-thirty. By leaving the 'afters' we were just able to catch the non-stop train back, which contrived to stop between stations. It is this sort of thing which has cut my week-end trips down to a minimum, and I'm not all that keen on a day out in the country either unless some kind friend is willing to transport me there and, far more important, will guarantee to get me back.

This sort of expedition can be highly enjoyable though, particularly if it is a rainy day. In that case there is no danger of the host or hostess saying, 'Let's go for a walk' or 'Let's get up an appetite before din-din', which ends in tears usually. One is dragged off whimpering like a child, sometimes chided for lagging behind, and certainly reaping the full benefit of the un-suitable clothes one has worn. One usually returns to London with a severe cold and a fairly heavy cleaners' bill.

I am willing to concede (very generous of you, Bull) that country air is better than the filthy stuff we breathe on our roofs in London, but what about the engine or motor fumes we breathe reaching the beautiful ozone in the depths of ? It's six of one and at least half a dozen of the other: Anyhow, there I am on my roof-top in swinging King's Road, enjoying the sun, and the phone goes and country folk are on the blower. 'You must come down,' they coo. 'It's lovely here,' and I say, 'Ta, ever so but it's lovely here too.' I then pop up on the roof again. It's always nice to be asked ANYWHERE, except possibly Cleveland, Ohio, but how can one explain one's perverted feelings to one's friends. I can't pretend that the view is exquisite from my roof, but the sky looks roughly the same everywhere. The towers of the Brompton Oratory and the Victoria and Albert Museum look Eastern enough if you half close your eyes. I can arrange an extension to the telephone and endless ice cubes, and when there is no wind it is just possible to carry on a fairly intelligent con-versation with the projectionists at the Chelsea Odeon (née

Gaumont) across the street. If my guests are so inclined they can catch fascinating glimpses of the denizens of the area by using binoculars.

I can't think what this chapter's about. I suppose all this preamble is pure filibustering in order to avoid telling my beloved friends who live in the country and you why I consider my sojourns in Greece so completely a different affair.

The basic reason, I imagine, is that it is my house—To Spiti Mou, I mean. I'm used to the beds and the geography of the house, and I have My Things around me. I also have a fairly regular number of friends coming and going and that has made the entire difference to my life out there. Although the place has magic, I still don't quite understand why they come in the first instance but I am deeply grateful that they brave the long journey and are willing to share the undoubted discomforts. I try to be totally undemanding but I think it is probably about the most selfish type of unselfishness. You have heard enough of the inconveniences of The Bullings and visitors are made just as conscious of them from the moment they arrive. It is best to brief them just after they've appreciated the view for the first time. It is then that I take the starlight out of their peepers by telling them about the disposal of the paper in the loo, which can easily land one up the well-known creek, if one isn't careful. I follow that up with the Non-Waste of Water lecture, which crumbles some of the more hygienic American visitors, with their mania for personal freshness and washing salads. To do them justice, a few days on Paxos reduces them to beachcomber status and cleaning habits of a lifetime are thrown into the Ionian. But there is a purity of air around that relaxes, and it is very difficult to get tetchy or short with anyone out there. A guest has to rely on his own resources for a lot of the time and as long as he or she has brought plenty of reading material or canvases or sheets of music, he or she is drachmae in. Guests also observe that their pig of a host is really doing exactly what he likes and they usually follow suit. And herein lies the secret. For as long as neither host nor guest feels any obligation or responsibility it is bound to work. But these circumstances are rare, however sensitive and understanding all parties are.

The struggle to see that the guest is never bored is, I think, a fruitless one sometimes, and there are lots of things more wasteful and destructive than boredom. In Paxos I am so bored sometimes that it actually becomes a pleasure to sit down and put this rubbish on a typewriter. And boredom at its best is one of the reasons why I go there. I find it impossible to do one creative thing while I'm in London and I am so undisciplined that I cannot write while the telephone or the front bell is liable to distract me. In a minute or two I will tell you of the temptations that beset me in my Greek isle but, at the risk of being platitudinous, the contrast between life there and in the King's Road is breath-taking. It is the feeling of freedom from responsibility and social guilt that makes it such a rest from the pace of existence in London and New York, where I've been lucky enough to spend the remainder of my time recently. I fear I sound like the late Elsa Maxwell or the current Duke and Duchess of Bedford, but you know what I mean. It's not that I go whirring round the night-clubs but I just like seeing my friends fairly regularly. To me continuity in a relationship is the most important (certainly the most rewarding) thing in my life. And as a result time is all too short for anything else. I think possibly I have lost all sense of proportion about this, as more and more I have pushed career (Ha! Ha!), possessions and certainly my wardrobe into the background, in that order of precedence. This is arrant nonsense really, I suppose, because perhaps I've never cared all THAT about any of them. I remember someone writing in my first autograph book: 'From quiet homes and first beginning, Out to the undiscovered ends, There's nothing worth the wear of winning But laughter and the love of friends.' And for me that is absolutely true.

The funny thing is that when I first went out to Paxos I thought it would not only be good for me but enjoyable to live alone for longish stretches at a time. And it was the collapse of this theory which was to give such a shock to my system. I find that after three days of my own company I'm absolutely SICK of myself and take every opportunity of going down to the village and having an ouzo or two with the inhabitants. I find that around two-thirty I have the telescope at the ready to check on the incoming ferry-boat for a possible unexpected visitor.

You may not believe it but I am convinced that I work better if there is someone there, ready to be impressed (or to pretend to be) by my industry. The moment they arrive they spur me on by their solicitude. 'We don't want to interfere with your work,' they say. 'What is your schedule?' I find myself inventing a tissue of lies but keeping to it. The moment they have gone the 'schedule' goes to pot and I am back devising the usual ingenious means for avoiding the actual 'pleasures of creation'.

Having lived in a fantasy world for the last fifty-five extremely odd years, I suppose it's perfectly natural for me to realize at this late date that there is absolutely no chance now of my ever being able to overcome my natural genius for self-deception. I use the word 'genius' with no sense of arrogance, as I realize that self-deception is the only quality I possess to a larger degree than most of my fellow creatures. Take for example phrases which are rarely off my lips:

'I love writing,' I say.

'Oh, yes,' I go on, 'I like it much more than acting.'

'I intend to devote most of my remaining years to writing.'

Note *en passant* (in passing) the nauseating self-satisfied use of the word 'devote'. I find myself going purple in the face with embarrassment as I type these pronunciamentos, knowing how wildly untrue they are. Am I calling me a liar? Yes, as a matter of fact, I am.

You see, all this carry-on about being a Writer is lunatic talk for a start. There is hardly a person living who isn't a prospective writer, except those who can't actually form the words, but even they could talk into machines and probably will. But most people jot things down on paper without any fuss whereas I bang on about it being such a Satisfying Experience.

Yet, in fact, between you and me and not on the whole the

spirit guide of the late Frank Harris, as far as I am concerned, Acting with a capital A is child's play compared with Getting Things Down On Paper, and I've come to dread the sight of the foolscap or quarto staring me reproachfully in the eye.

'Don't just sit there. Use us for heaven's sake,' they seem to say with those dreadful blank white faces.

In London, as I've hinted, it is hideously easy to avoid facing up to things like Getting into a Routine for Writing a Book. There are so many splendid but inescapable diversions like the laundry, having a bath, answering the telephone, coping with the mail and going down several flights of stairs (and up again) to deal with the front-door bell. So it has become an established fact at the back of my mind that when I go to Greece I go there principally to Write. I've even convinced the front of my mind. When asked why I have built a house in such a remote spot I find myself answering: 'In order to write, silly.'

'Oh, what a good idea!' says Silly. 'It must be very easy for you out there. It's so quiet.'

I smile at the sillies happily and in a hopefully calculated way which should convince them of my extreme dedication to my craft. But 'craft' is the operative word and I wish they could catch me on Paxos thinking out new crafty excuses to avoid putting my fingers on the typewriter. I know I don't mean to be so undisciplined and most night-times I am filled with good resolutions for the morrow. If I am alone at The Bullings I retire early (nine-thirtyish) in order to be Fresh as a Daisy in the morning. I rise at five-thirty and (I know you will be unable to believe this) I can sometimes spin things out so that I don't actually sit down to Creation until nine-thirty. It is a major triumph for the Potterer and I don't mean One who makes Pots. Only my factotum, Alekkos, is likely to disturb me during the day with goods, mail or water, and that won't be till dusk. But it is vastly reassuring to see how many useless things I can find to occupy me from the moment I rise from my bed.

I can, for instance, spread the bedclothes round the garden to air them. This takes quite a lot out of me as they have to be suspended from olive-trees or pinned down on Mr Ypsilos's rocks. Then I turn the mattress and sweep out the corpses of moths, wasps, bees, caterpillars, mosquitoes which Aerosol makes short shrift of last thing at night. All this activity takes place in the Guest Room, which is the Host Room when I'm on my own. Next I go into the main Living Area, open the windows and put the kettle on for the eight cups of Instant Maxwell Maison which I'll consume in the morning to Pull Myself Together.

What's next on the Agenda for Filibustering? Oh yes, find out how The World is getting on. I switch on the radio and get the 0400 Greenwich Mean Time news. I don't think we have Mean Time in Greece. There is a sense of Suspended Time, which is unique; and, though I know it sounds the peak of affectation, it is quite a major problem sometimes to work out what day of the week it is; I've noticed newcomers nonplussed and angry by being suddenly shaken by uncertainty and argument on the subject.

The English radio gives me the Test Match score and says how lovely the weather is over there (here in Paxos it's been Mistrals and Thunderstorms on and off for days), and I switch over to The Voice of America station, which tends to be a tidge too hysterical for me first thing in the ack emma. At one time there didn't seem to be a single peaceful area in the globe because American Marines had landed Everywhere to 'Protect' someone or other. But, however bad the news, it is interspersed with a great many scrummy records by Count Basie, Duke Ellington, Earl Sammy Davis Junior, Lena Horne, Ella Fitzgerald, Louis Armstrong, Nat King Cole and Peggy Lee. I imagine this selection is to impress the Overseas listener with the current liberality of the Nation on the Civil Rights issue. Miss Lee is thrown in occasionally to please the coloured folk listening, which includes me after a few weeks in the sun.

A far less attractive feature of The Voice of America, so far as I am concerned, is the Daily Scientific Fact with which this station tries to cram my poor brain. It is dished out (sponsored is the word I wasn't looking for) by an organ called the *Lockheed*

Digest, with a well-informed gent called Orville Anderson 'reporting' in that maddening-type voice which made the Fitzpatrick Travelogues so deeply unattractive vocally.

In any case a Daily Scientific Fact is the last thing I want to assimilate in uptown Lakka. The World of Science has encroached on us very little here and my Gas Fridge and Flushing Loo are regarded as very advanced indeed. Television is happily practically unheard of and all the information the inhabitants seem to require from Radio Kerkyra, the local station, is the local weather report to see if it is going to be propitious (a) for fishing and (b) for shooting trigonia, those poor little turtle-doves which shelter on the island waiting for visas to emigrate. The shooting season is mercifully short and I cannot pretend that bits of shrapnel whistling past one's ear should prevent a genuinely creative artist from Having a Bash, and in any case I could move indoors to avoid a stray bullet putting paid to my chef d'oeuvre.

So I have to think of other excuses for not starting work yet. I am quite suddenly ravenous and cook myself a gargantuan fry-up. This takes up the best part of half an hour with the washing up, and indeed the washing down (more coffee). There is a little hot water over, so I take the opportunity to wash out some tea towels (dishcloths or what have you? Well, what HAVE you?) in something called ROL, and the entire building is now as spick-and-span as it's likely to be.

It's too early and I'm certainly too greedy to start thinking about lunch so what else craves my attention?

The garden! But, of course. I empty a bit more of the last guest's last hot water-bottle over the Morning Glory seeds, a recent addition to To Spiti Mou, which I have planted in order to cater for needy drug addicts if and when they arrive. The occasional poppies which have appeared will give additional variety to them and they should all be as merry and stoned as grigs in no time. I shall leave the other plants till dusk as they aren't so frail and are eight in number.

Ah, the ants are out and about in the morning sunshine so we can cry halt to the overnight truce. I usually start the morning by peeing on the two most threatening Ant Heaps in the area. The creatures aren't all that keen on this gesture but then they prefer it to the Ordeal by Fire to which I subject them frequently. This consists of putting a ring of petrol round them and down their holes, if you know what I mean, and setting fire to the whole caboodle. This should spread alarm and despondency in the Ant City, but the lull only lasts a day and then representatives come up to the surface to reconnoitre and one starts the whole thing over again. I try variations and I must admit that, unlike the average Greek housewife, ants loathe ROL and TRYL, the two washing liquids. So most bowls of dirty washing-up water go straight on to the ants, who I'm sure keep spotless establishments and don't want any interference in their personal hygiene.

I am in the middle of forcing one army of ants into a strategic withdrawal when I hear the tooting of The Pullman and I have to dash inside to get my props to carry out the embarrassing performance which I have described in another chapter and don't intend to put either of us through again. But it takes a bit of time and there will be a second showing when the ferry-boat leaves Lakka and is Corfu-bound.

And now it is the Moment of Truth. Because after the ferry has gone beyond communication distance I shall have to sit down at the wash-stand which serves as my desk. The little ledge at the back prevents the blank pages from blowing away (in theory). So armed with everything I could conceivably need for the rest of the morning I disconsolately take up my creative position. Flanked by chairs which carry dictionaries, lexicons, rubbers, combs, a telescope and some Nivea cream, I sit praying for yet another miraculous diversion. There is regrettably no chance of another Eclipse. Goodness THAT was a lovely time-waster!

I had actually started work on that particular morning but for once seemed to have missed out on the news as my radio appeared to be on the blink and I was saving the batteries. Around eleven o'clock, when the sun had reached full strength and was blazing away, I felt a sudden chill in the air. I had been sitting under an olive-tree so I moved out into the blazing sun. The curious thing was that it was not blazing hot. It was blazing cold, a phenomenon that even I noticed.

I went and put a woolly on and went on sitting in what should have been the heat of the midday sun. The sky started to go darker though there wasn't a cloud in the sky. I knew that this wasn't quite right and for the only time in my life I wouldn't have minded having Orville Anderson and the whole staff of the *Lockheed Digest* standing by me. I thought I'd take a peek at the silly old sun through my telescope, though I gathered subsequently that this action might have affected me eyes-wise. 'Eyes-wise!' What a repellent phrase! It sounds like a small girl being cute and wildly sexy, with a lolly in her mouth and a provocative smile on her lips. Anyhow I looked through my telescope and there were the sun and moon at it like knives, my dears. Suddenly I had a mental flashback to the carry-on at Winchester Coll just the forty years ago when we were all given bits of cardboard with round black filters on them to study a Total Eclipse.

So I put away the telescope and went into the house to fetch a few of the pairs of sun-glasses which forgetful guests have left there over the years. Through these I scientifically studied the situation. After a short but thorough scrutiny it became as clear as daylight. Paxos was in the throes of an Eclipse. Pleased at my sensational discovery I studied the implications happily till it was time to serve myself a light luncheon.

Today the sky looks v. uneclipsy (derived from the Greek, 'ekleepsis'. Is that not interesting? Yes, that is not interesting) and there's nothing to prevent me from ending this chapter and starting on the next.

'Where's the paper?'

'No, I can't have.'

'Oh, how awful.'

'I've run out. And there's none in Lakka. I shan't be able to get cracking until I get some from Corfu.'

'What a disaster!'

'Oh, lawks!'

9. *Hot Running Waiter*

To the north-east of Corfu (I mean in this case the capital and not the island), roughly twelve kilometres away, lies the spread-out village of Ypsos, part of which faces the sea at a few paces. Quite apart from being the home of my friend Nikos Kaloudis it is notable for an extraordinary drama which has developed over a number of years on what can be described as the sea front. Here are situated side by side two hotels called Costas and Mega.

At first sight, or indeed second and fifteenth, they appear to be the same building. For some unknown reason the word 'Costas' is nowhere displayed prominently whereas 'Mega' is clearly visible. I have remonstrated with Vassilys Zavropopoulos, the proprietor of Costas, about this and his explanation, like so many of his utterances, makes no sense at all. I point out that eager customers sometimes go whizzing by because they can't see any sign up and on their return pop into the Mega. It is at this point that Vassilys pretends not to be listening because it is his Worst Thing: mention of the word 'Mega'. In fact he's tried to exorcise it from his vocabulary.

'What is mega, please?' he will say to me. 'Don't understand what you are speaking.' And so on.

From the road the two hotels appear to have identical obvious assets. Both have terraces right on the water, with small jetties for boats, swimming and sunbathing. Both have plenty of bedrooms looking on to the sea and fine parking places for cars. Both have good kitchens though Vassilys tends to whisper the menu into the customers' ears 'In case,' he says, with a baleful look across the way at the Mega, 'anyone hears.' I might very easily not have gone to Costas if I hadn't been recommended to it by Marie Aspioti of Corfu Travel Ltd, and if things had turned out differently I might, I only say might, have been writing all this from a Mega Point of View and not that of Costas.

For some reason or other I originally arrived at Costas by sea and I do remember that it was more than dodgy. Missing slats in the jetty presented serious hazards to me and it wasn't until I got ashore that I realized we had set off for the Dancing at Barbardy from this identical spot the year before. The whole Zavropopoulos family welcomed me ashore warmly, giving me every assistance, as well they might. I discovered later I was the only guest in their hotel and they would have been ill-advised to lose me in the sea before I had registered.

I got to know the Zs pretty well over the next few weeks as I was constantly going into huddles with them and Nikos, who lived within a fairly long stone's throw inland. The father, Costas by name, had died only recently, having built up a steady holiday trade from the Corfiotes. The tourists hadn't yet filtered through much, thank heaven. Public transport was (and indeed is) still pretty disgraceful in this particular area and out of season (up to mid-June and from September onwards) the first bus for Ypsos leaves at 1.30 in the afternoon, and if you want to get back to the capital that night you have to catch THE bus back at 5.30. And, as the two hotels have little to offer in the way of entertainment in the evening it is not wildly attractive to the usual tourist to stay in them until more variety is at hand. For the kinky there is certainly enough. Just to hear the phonograph concerts during an average evening is nectar to me. If the Mega is on a classical binge, Vassilys is rummaging in his collection for the

latest jazz. The noise can be deafening and sometimes drives me half-way up the mountain behind the hotels.

Vassilys, the senior brother, is the man in charge, and very droll and interesting he is. Tall for a Greek, he has a crew-cut and a fairly haphazard knowledge of the English language. But, goodness, how he tries to master it! There was an occasion, for instance, when I was helping him construct a prospectus for the hotel. Poised with pencil and paper he was having a real bash.

'English library,' he announced, with a sideways look at me.

'If you feel yourself justified in calling an old James Bond, a map of Paris for 1926 and a dirty Spanish book with a torn cover showing a lady in black knickers an English library, yes, Vassilys, of course,' I said stuffily, 'but it's up to your conscience.'

He wavered and then wrote down 'library', naked and unashamed.

'Running hot and cold water,' he continued.

'No, Vassilys,' I said firmly.

He looked very hurt.

'Cold running water,' I continued, 'there is spasmodically, but there is no question and never has been of hot running water.'

'But,' said Vassilys, 'if I send Antonio the waiter running with the hot water it will be hot running water.'

'You mean hot running waiter with the hot running water.'

'Yes, Mr Peeetsa,' said Vassilys, and leaned back roaring with laughter for about half an hour. So I told him to put it on the prospectus. I hasten to add for prospective clients that there is now both hot and cold running water all over the place and even through the showers, though in the case of the latter one has to be extremely mobile as Vassilys obviously used a dwarf as a model and one has to get into a series of complicated and humiliating positions in order to derive any benefit from this form of cleansing.

On the back of the door in every room there is an extremely long document giving details of prices, rules, etc. At Costas a 'Hot Bath in Public Bathroom' costs twelve drachmae, which is one-third of the cost of a whole day's lodging. The document

omits to say what a Hot Bath in Private Bathroom would cost but as there is actually only one fairly Private Shower I suppose it doesn't matter much.

But then a great deal of what is presented so officially is just plain gibberish. Take, for example, this specimen of the Tourist Office's command of English:

'In the case that only 1 person stays is a two or three Beeldret room the charge is for 1 bed only. If the client asks that no one is admitted in the room is obliged to pay the charge for all beds of the room.'

In actual fact, if you just change the first 'is' into 'in' and 'beeldret' into 'bedroom', it means that if you refuse to let every Tom, Dick and indeed Harry into your room you will be forced to pay for all the beds in the room, and, lawks-a-mussy, you have no idea how many beds the Greeks can get into a room if pressed.

The notice goes on to say 'The client of an hotel has the right to make use of the room up to 14th hours. Staying over the 18th hour binds the client to payment of the whole sum fixed for a day's rent.' What confuses me more than somewhat is what happens in between the 14th and 18th. This seems to me to be a limbo time in which anything might happen. One suddenly has a terrific shock when one reads that the service charge appears to be 1500, which seems an awful lot until one realizes that this particular firm of printers has no '%' to its name unlike Messrs Morrison and Gibb Limited who are dealing with this load of rubbish.

Costas Hotel makes one more wildly optimistic pronunciamento: 'When heating or cooling is provided by individual units the client is not obliged to pay for it if he does not want it.'

When I asked Vassilys where his 'individual units' were he roared with laughter in my face. He has very few illusions about the amenities of his hotel and all he asks is that the traveller or tourist should treat him as a friend. By a freak of chance, some years ago in an article in the *Sunday Express*, I was able to draw attention to Costas Hotel and as a result a certain amount of trade came trickling his way from England. Albert Finney, Susannah

York, Paul Scofield and his family, Harry Andrews, Sybil Christopher (Burton as was) and various other theatricals popped in and were pretty entranced by the atmosphere. Vassilys pretended to be totally unimpressed and all he wanted to know about them was what they thought of (a) his English and (b) his Crème Caramel. As regards the first we were all fairly dotty about a card he sent out at the festive season. It was printed and said 'Mary Christmas' as if it was a lady, and underneath it was 'Much love Vassilys'. Sometimes at Christmas there is a photograph of the hotel. I know that is what it is meant to be but it is only visible through a forest of trees and it looks like a derelict building which has not been touched for over a century. In order to confuse everyone there is often a boat in the foreground which has nothing to do with anything, except I know the gent in it has a high falsetto which goes ill with his rough exterior.

But Vassilys rarely makes the same mistake twice and he now has a rather swinging prospectus and a steady flow of regular clients who appear to stay beyond the 18th hour.

The food, which is consistently good, is in the hands of his brother Andreas. He also is open to suggestions and only wants you to eat what you fancy. When N. was there he liked to have his eggs fried BOTH sides (you know what Americans are like) and Andreas just handed over the pan to him and watched fascinated.

Mrs Zavropopoulos remains very much in the background and lets her sons get on with it. She is a handsome dignified lady who tends to wear the National Costume which includes that effective head-covering which seems to be contrived out of a series of handkerchiefs. I took some friends out there to lunch and one of them was riveted by this article of clothing. Not surprising as it was Margaret Furse who had won an Oscar that year for her designs for the costumes in *Becket*. She was there with her husband, Stephen Watts, and her first husband, Roger Furse, who illustrated this book, to make it even more confusing. And to simplify things she was called Watts before she married either of them. Anyhow she hissed at me, pointing at Mrs Z.'s top-knot: 'Do you think she'd show me how she does it?'

I explained the situation to Vassilys who spoke briefly to his Mum. She smiled at Maggie and we all went into the kitchen where she unwound the head-dress until her hair fell around her shoulders. She explained the whole thing to Maggie in mime and then re-dressed her hair. When she'd covered her head again she invited us, through her son, to have a drink with her. It was oddly moving, for suddenly she was queenlike in her dignity. Normally she rarely issues forth from the kitchen and until recently a look of sheer terror used to come into her face when I advanced on her on my first visit of the season. She really shrank and, for heaven's sake, why shouldn't she? Now she seems more prepared for the inevitable and gives a faint smile as I go towards her. But it doesn't prevent a wincette or bijou wince when I actually kiss her.

I often wonder what Mrs Zavropopoulos thinks of the feud that has grown up between the hotel her husband started and the Mega next door. For it is this which highlights life around here. If the Mega has the impertinence to add a few feet on to her jetty one day it is safe to predict that Costas's ditto will be similarly and slightly more endowed shortly. A row of flowerpots on Costas's balcony will bring forth window-boxes on the Mega's terrace. The rivalry during 'the season' is intense. Yet, apart from the cocks, cats and lizards who cross the boundary at whim, there is no communication between the two buildings unless one or the other runs out of bread. Each pretends that its rival simply doesn't exist. Yet if I had gone to the Mega in the first place I am sure I should have been as loyal to them as I am to Costas. It always SEEMS a nice establishment and the staff have an excellent sense of humour. I recall an incident which has now passed into Corfu folklore.

Sometimes, egged on by Vassilys, I used to sit near the road stuffing myself with food, to attract passing trade. I never thought this device wildly successful as I imagine most discerning persons thought how frightfully unappetizing the whole thing looked. But on one particular occasion there was no need to attract customers. It was a Sunday and Costas was jammed. In fact I was having considerable trouble in getting a cup of tea (tsai). I grabbed at waiters' coats, clapped my hands and pretended to cry. But they were all too busy with gargantuan and tardy lunches and finally I got up, stepped across the little wall into the Mega and sat down at one of the tables on their terrace.

'Tsai. Tsai. Tsai,' I said in a loud clear voice.

A waiter who had been watching the goings-on at Costas with the keenest interest brought me three cups of tea immediately.

The affair became the Joke of the Neighbourhood and I still find comparative strangers stopping dead in their tracks on seeing me and saying, 'Tsai. Tsai. Tsai,' which confuses anyone who happens to be with me at the time. But I shall be enormously flattered if fifty years hence one person in the Ypsos neighbourhood remembers the story, even if he gets it all wrong.

Hereabouts legends have a habit of sticking and I particularly like the one about the restaurateur, Mr Pipillas, an elderly Greek, who with his wife kept a modest eating-house in a small village called Kondakali, about half-way to Ypsos from the capital. He built up a very fine reputation and Corfiotes came from all over the island to sample his fish dishes. One day some guests arrived and Mr Pipillas was delighted to be told afterwards that one of them had been a princess of Greece with some friends. A year later he was getting ready for a jolly good fry-up when the King and Queen clocked in for lunch. Mr Pipillas seated them and asked them what they'd like.

'Ah,' said the King, 'that's for you to decide. I've been told that the eating here is pretty good.'

Mr Pipillas bustled about and served what he thought might appeal to his royal customers. At the end of the meal His Majesty sent for Mr Pipillas and told him that it was just about the best meal he remembered partaking of. Mr Pipillas went back into the kitchen on wings and told Mrs Pipillas what the King had said to him. Mrs Pipillas just had time to say 'Tee aurea' (How lovely!) when Mr Pipillas had a stroke and died. Not a bad way to go, eh?

The food at Costas is pretty good too, though I wish they

wouldn't keep an enormous octopus continuously in the deep-freeze. I dread seeing it and occasionally have nightmares during the course of which It chases me up the stairs. On the other hand I can really forgive them anything because of the exquisite crème caramels that come out of that kitchen. Vassilys sometimes sends me a consignment over to Paxos accompanied by some of his own excellent wine. Indeed they are so generous that I find it impossible to keep pace. Half the things aren't even entered on an ordinary meal bill and cups of coffee and ouzos are dished out regardless. As I keep on saying, I am sure it would be the same at the Mega. But how to find out is the problem. My only contact there has now, alas, departed.

She was an exquisite old English lady, called, I think, Miss Peach, who was around the ninety mark. She spent every spring at the Mega gathering spring flowers. She wore floppy old-fashioned mob caps and seemed very strong for one looking so frail. She climbed great hills and went on picnics, always returning with a beautiful bunch of rare specimens, which she put in a glass and studied during the next meal. She gave me the most awful lambasting for not mentioning the Mega in my article in the *Sunday Express*. She appeared to take it as a personal affront, for had she not chosen the hotel herself, and the people were so delightful that it was tantamount to a crime to hurt their feelings. I felt awful and swore to her that I'd remedy it somehow. Till now I've done nothing about it. But the following year she came up to me one day and said how pleased she'd been to hear that I had spoken highly about the Mega. Where she had got this misinformation from I wouldn't know, but I confess that I didn't disillusion her. So wherever you are, dear little Miss Peach, here with my love are my amends. I AM SURE THE MEGA IS A LOVELY HOTEL. I would not know personally because, if I set foot on their threshold the Zavropopoulos's would be out in their threes, armed to the hilt. But I shall go on patronizing Costas myself so as to be sure of a Good Laugh. Even though Vassilys doesn't mind being sent up about his hotel (I once said in print that his beds were super for those suffering from sciatica), he loves it and is very proud of it. He also doesn't believe that his guests should have everything their own way.

'Peetsa,' he said the other day, 'shall I put a notice up in the room saying "The Customer is Always Wrong"?'

'I don't think it would actually encourage trade,' I replied. 'A lot of dreary people might not think it very funny.'

When I had explained what 'dreary' meant, he said: 'But, Peetsa, I don't want dreary people, I want only jokesy people like you and your friends.'

Dear Vassilys, I hope he gets enough of them. Though perhaps I worry too much about him. This year on my first visit I got near the Mega and saw the terrace crammed with tables, obviously in preparation for some Sunday wedding party. My heart sank. I thought, 'Poor Vassilys. He'll die of jealousy.'

I needn't have worried. In front of Costas and spreading over the road and practically up the staircase were more decorated tables than at the Mega. Whether anyone was actually going to turn up was another matter.

10. *The Homecoming*

The saying, 'There's No Place Like Home', is absolute rubbish to me now that I have my little Greek House. It's exactly like home as a matter of fact. In addition, it may be the comparative novelty of it all or the secret feeling of One-upmanship that is unavoidable, but I now feel far more emotional when I return to To Spiti Mou than I do when I clock in at my flat in the King's Road, Chelsea, London, Great Britain, the Western Hemisphere, etc. It's not that I love the latter any less, with its happy associations, and bulging at the seams with My Things. It's just that every time I see it after a longish absence I am very conscious of the changes that are going on all around the poor little thing. It makes me nervous as, with all the construction and destruction taking place in the area, it is difficult to believe that anything of a certain age (including the inhabs) will be allowed to remain standing for more than ten years at most.

I have a recurring nightmare that I shall get back from some trip to foreign parts and find no trace of my London residence. It is all very vivid and everyone else is exactly where they were before but they survey me with blank faces and politely tell me that I must have made a mistake as they have never seen me in all their puffs. It's not a frightfully attractive or restful dream, and it resembles *The Lady Vanishes* and *So Long at the Fair*, except that in my case I can find no one to have faith in my story that I do actually live in a flat above Mr Kent, the tobacconist, sweet shop and toyshop. I wake up sweating and insecure.

None of these feelings are helped by the Press, and indeed everyone, saying how London is changing. It is beyond a joke to come back from the mad rush and pressure of New York to find that, seemingly overnight, the English capital has become 'The Swinging City of the World'. I thought to find the whole place in violent motion and people swaying back and forth, like you see at revivalist meetings when I first read that. I pictured a sort of Fellini-type background and a lot of mid-air stuff. The more adventurous Swingers would, I was certain, trapes on trapezes from party to orgy and vice versa.

It has got pretty close to that, funnily enough, and the King's Road of a Saturday afternoon has a Babylonian atmosphere which I am sure would have pleased the late D. W. Griffith. This situation has interfered rather seriously with my funeral plans. You see, I made my will for the umpteenth time the other day and, when the kindly lawyer asked me about the disposal of my remains, I suggested, quite honestly, that I would like my ashes to be scattered over the King's Road on a Saturday when a large percentage of chums would be shopping or showing off. Not that I wanted a fragment of me to strike a chum in the face but it was a way of showing how happy I had been in the area for so many years. I'm afraid I would just have to risk not lodging in an eye and causing extreme pain to a Passer-By.

Anyhow that was my simple plan for my last appearance in the S.W.3. postal area, but Mr Niekirk (of Bull and Bull, Solicitors; advt because they aren't allowed to do so: advertise I mean) put the kibosh on everything by saying he thought it would be impossible to carry out my wishes as there was a law prohibiting this type of exhibitionism over crowded thorough-fares.

I was about to suggest that the Scattering should take place at night when I realized that, in the light of this new Sodom and

Gomorrah (what did THEY do?) plus the oo-la-la-oui-oui reputation of Jolly Old Londres c'est très gai, it might be difficult to find a suitable location. Certainly the new building at the corner of Markham Square could provide a Bank (Barclays) on which the Wild Thyme might not only blow but also be joined by my ashes and the three pounds odd that I still have deposited there.

But at night-time I suppose even business premises are attacked by the Swinging Element and become 'crowded thoroughfares'. In any case it would be frightfully embarrassing for all parties, particularly those in progress at the time, and not least for the Spirit-Guide of the deceased, if he found himself (like the Wild Thyme) blowing right back in the faces of those attempting to bring back Licence, Lechery and Lust to Lovely Lazy London.

So, as a result of all the afore-mentioned complications, I have decided to entrust my mortal remains to the stony ground outside To Spiti Mou. I shall at any rate upset no one there and rest remarkably content in the knowledge that I can watch, in sort of person, the pleasure and love I've received from the small property rising phoenix-like around my ashes, and multiplying. Some of you may find the whole of the preceding passages in bad taste and I apologize if that is so. But to me, at the moment, after a happy and seemingly incredibly lucky life, death has no special fears. And as regards the island of Paxos being the most suitable place to end up in, I am perfectly serious. Because whatever guided me there in the first place has followed through with a continuity of near-perfection.

'Goodness the way he bangs on!' I can hear you say and you are right. But, as I have endeavoured to point out, security and lack of change are now at a premium all over the world. And it is only in the remoter spots that there is any hope of their being maintained. In my tiny Eden however I cannot see any major alterations in the foreseeable future. Any additions or amendments will be my own doing and will probably be connected with an attempt to improve either the comfort or practicality of the property.

The whole point is that on my annual return to To Spiti Mou I have not the slightest fear that I shall not find everything exactly as it was when I last saw it. I can be certain that the quantity of the precious Worcester sauce on the shelf will have remained constant and that the oil-lamps will all be trimmed, cleaned, and ready for action. The gas cylinders will be attached to the refrigerator and the stove so that I can start operating in the kitchen on arrival. Alekkos will point with pride at the huge pile of laundered linen that his wife has done and at the rugs on the floor, all of which have been cleaned. Floors will have been scrubbed and the loo will appear ready to be flushed.

In fact the whole building looks a treat. Outside there are disappointments but I have learned to expect them. Why, for instance, hasn't the one surviving vine grown through the winter so that by now it is covering the roof, bulging with great clusters of grapes? The geraniums haven't spread all over the stone wall as I had hoped and my one bean plant hasn't produced a family. To compensate, perhaps, some strangers have popped up. A small cluster of pea-stalks and a beautiful display of poppies under one of my vines. Alekkos has planted (I suspect the very morning of my arrival) a few shoots of bright orange nasturtiums to provide 'a show'. And heaven knows we need one, for it must be admitted, quite apart from the greedy depravity of the goats of the neighbourhood, the earth hereabouts is a stinker, being of rocky temperament and as dry as cement, and in actual fact laced with it, cement I mean. This year Geoffrey Toone bravely planted an army of seeds, including morning glory, which would have helped any drug fiends who happened to pop in for a short stay. But some weeks after, while I was away, ghastly goats descended in hoards and ate everything they could lay their beastly beards on.

Only the basilikos has survived and entirely through another guest's courage. Barry Justice went pretty berserk about this herb, and two pots of it were presented to us, which meant that everything except boiled eggs was lavishly sprinkled with it. Barry, a v. good cook, decided to take one of the plants home, which survived a trip on an overcrowded boat to Patras, a jerky and frightening ride to Athens on a bus driven by a young speed-maniac, and a night in a bidet in a sleazy hotel in the capital. The Customs officers in England ignored it and it is now cosseted daily in Mr Justice's Belgravia hide-out. Every now and again I go round there on a Basil Jag.

It wouldn't have lasted long in the Rock Garden at Lakka and until I build a fence or stone wall round my property I see no hope, horticulturally speaking. But you only have to get to the cliff-edge to look down on a carpet of yellow broom which takes your breath away. Throughout the summer the colours change but there is always something beautiful in view and my four olives are a permanent pleasure, beside providing essential shade.

Anyhow it is extremely difficult to take your eyes off the real magic: the blue-green sea, over a hundred feet down but with such clear water that you can hear the fish making their usual comments on my return.

'That old fat fool's back.'

'I know. I wonder what he'll send whizzing down over the cliff this year.'

'As long as it's not those dreary sardine tins. Even if there are a few bits left in them it's like bringing coals to Newcastle.' ('Ho Newcastle' in Greek.)

Across the bay everything is as it should be. There again are the ruined chapel on the opposite promontory and Ulysses' supposed petrified ship. I say 'supposed' because there are as many claimants to this relic as there are to Queen Elizabeth's or G. Washington's bed, King Arthur's Round Table, or, in the Corfu area, 'the house where the Durrells lived'. It is perfectly true that the family changed their abode a number of times when they were there in the thirties but I must have had at least twenty houses pointed out to me as genuine. And it did make me chortle when I was having dinner with rather a name-dropping occupant of an ex-Durrell house. He showed me with pride a pretty painted chest.

'That,' he said, 'is Margaret Durrell's painting-box.'

'Oh, yes,' I replied wittily.

The next day I happened to be lunching with Lawrence Durrell (who's name-dropping now?) and mentioned the incident. He said that his sister, to his fairly certain knowledge, at that time never put a paintbrush into her mitt.

Oh dear, I've strayed again and lost the Vista. But I seem to have got myself back to Corfu, which may be a good thing as I notice I've called this chapter 'The Homecoming' and it is in Corfu that this operation starts.

I have a very special affection for the larger Ionian island and I very rarely go straight on to Paxos, though with the London–Corfu direct flight this is now possible. But I prefer to spend a night or two in the capital city. It is a most attractive town with its strange mixture of Venetian, French and Byzantine architecture and I can wander happily through the cobbled streets and narrow thoroughfares where the tops of the houses are at hand-shaking distance from each other.

But, though by now I ought to know every foot of it, parts of Corfu are as complicated as Hampton Court maze and I still get totally lost looking for something like the Old Roman Well.

'You must know Corfu backwards,' say my friends.

'If I must, I must,' I reply dangerously, like the lady in that splendid short story by Saki who, when informed at some wayside station by a domineering matron that she must be the new governess, said that if she must be she must be. And indeed Was for the next few days because she had nothing more amusing to do at the time. Unlike her I end up lost, humiliated and a Figure of Fun, having totally failed to find the Roman or indeed any well.

But it is still splendid to set foot in Corfu as to me it represents the Gateway to Greece, being the nearest readily accessible part of the kingdom. I get imbued with the magic when I step off the plane and on to the tarmac. It's not only the sudden change in temperature and temperament, it's the tempo. After a few hours on Greek soil I am free from pressure and feel as if I'd never left.

It's not as if the country was impervious to change. No; unfortunately, with the immense sudden growth of the Tourist Industry, a revolution is taking place. Hotels and houses are being built at breakneck speed and projects of a grandiose nature are being embarked on regardless. Some of them are doomed to failure like the new theatre in Corfu, which I remember looking very imposing on my first visit some years back. Now the building is overgrown with some extremely pretty weeds and it is impossible to imagine that dear old Madame Paxinou will be able to bang away there for a decade or so. It is a huge edifice and was originally designed to be aligned with shops and terraces, but I gather that not only are the acoustic problems likely to prove insurmountable but also that it may very easily be pulled down before completion to make way for a smaller theatre!

In its early days apparently the theatre ran neck and neck with the sewers for preferential financial aid and I for one am grateful that the latter Stole a March, a theft which brings one naturally to a discussion of the Public Conveniences of the town. Although there is not a great deal of competition for the honour, there is no doubt as to the most attractive and original W.C. in Corfu.

It reposes underground on the Promenade, a short distance from the bandstand and is surrounded by grassy stretches. You go down a few steps (Ladies to the left and Gents to the right) and are greeted by the chirruping of canaries as you enter the portals. At least six cages full are suspended from the ceiling in each partition, and a pretty surprising sight they are. In the day-time, that is. Night comes and . . . well, you see, I was telling A. Finney about the birds and he simply wouldn't believe me, so I took him along one evening and to my horror they weren't in their customary position. And Mr F. said, there you are, exaggerating as usual, and I asked the dear little old man who looks after the loo where the little creatures were.

'Poo einai ta poulia;' I asked.

He led us to the inside cubicles where ta poulia were having a nice zizz. 'Peristero besikia edow,' (Quieter here) he said.

We didn't think it politic to ask what a late and possibly

drunken reveller would make of it if he found an inhabited birdcage where he wanted to sit. Anyhow, there you are, Birds at Your Convenience!

Horticulturists will probably be more interested in the W.C. by the Old Port which has a constant fine floral display both inside and out. But these are the only two specimens of the genre that I can confidently and currently recommend to customers. Some of the others are—oh, for heaven's sake let's get away from the Sanitary Situation to the Cultural. For instance, take the Museum. This building seems to have retrogressed a bit since last year, when it appeared almost ready to open its doors. Here again, as in the case of the theatre, there has, I believe, been financial difficulty, but by the time this tome has been published (and probably remaindered) the handsome modern building will have made itself available to eager visitors.

I have followed its progress with compulsory interest since the beginning, as it is situated exactly opposite the Hotel Calypso, the pretty little place where I am wont to stay. The last two years I have had no need of an alarm clock as the gents who have been working on the Museum start banging about (and I do mean banging about) at precisely 0700 hours. Quite apart from this diversion there is always plenty going on at the Calypso, even though it is tucked up a side street at the back of the swanky Corfu Palace. From quite a few of the front bedrooms it is perfectly possible to see and hear most of the film being shown at the Phoenix Open-Air Cinema. One's view of the screen is a trifle oblique but it is comparatively easy to space out one's evening so that one goes to dine just as the main feature is coming on again.

I'm sorry but I shouldn't have settled in at the Calypso without leaving the tarmac which I got off on several hundred words away. But I must not omit the essential features that make my return to Greece so nostalgic. With luck, as I get off the plane I am kissed by one of the excessively pretty young ladies who man Corfu airport. The one who may greet me in this flattering fashion is called Mary Sklevantis and she speaks perfect English.

Thanks mainly to Mary S. I am whisked through the Customs at outrageous speed and on a recent visit they didn't even bother to look at my new filter pump, which I carried over my shoulder as if it was a camera. A taxi takes me to the already much mentioned Calypso Hotel where the three maids greet me as if I was a Beatle. They are, in my opinion, entitled to be classed as sex-maniacs as only this type of person could really be seemingly consumed with desire for a very old stout party. To make it more confusing the trio have fine serious foreheads and could have stepped either right into or out of the chorus of the *Medea*. There was once a production of this jolly piece in London when some of the ladies of the chorus got so bored that they used to play noughts and crosses on the dust of the stage with their feet. But the Calypso girls are less frivolous and their fixed stares and extraordinary habit of opening doors when one hasn't a stitch on are disconcerting to say the least of it. But acceptance of this frank and unusual behaviour has its compensations, particularly when one wants to get the laundry done swiftly and efficiently, even if returned with a generous supply of leers and light caresses.

After unpacking I lock away anything which might unduly excite the girls. Otherwise they tend to brood over snaps and go through one's personal effects like rats up drainpipes and leave anything they think sexy displayed obviously on top.

I realize that I have written the saga of the Calypso Maidens in the present tense and I now have to confess to those sex-maniac devotees who are already thinking of booking in, that the girls are in the past, though possibly now disturbing some other hostelry. The new proprietors of the Calypso have wisely engaged some steady but elderly maids who make life for everyone a tidge easier. But I am still just starting on my home-coming so you must make allowances for the time-lag and the tense changes and accompany me to the post office, which is the most vital building in Corfu as far as I am concerned. It is staffed by a mixture of some of the most helpful and most maddening people in the town. There is one character in the telephone and telegraphic department who disappears for hours to some

unknown dream world of his own, though he has your instructions in his hand, made out in Greek and English. Precious hours
tick by while he stares in front of him and I would love to know
where he goes in his trance. There is also a totally blind man who
does up your parcels, after you have undone them to show the
contents. You finally have to go to his assistance, which is in my
case the perfect example of the blind helping the blind. It is a
major operation to obtain stamps in Paxos so I purchase vast
quantities of every denomination. I also pass the time of day
with Poste Restante to make certain that it knows that I am in
the area and won't send all my mail hurtling back to London,
as so often happens while I am quietly in Paxos.

From the G.P.O. I stroll through the main shopping area,
noticing the number of buildings which have sprung up in the
past year (surely the Olympic Hotel is new?) and I pluck a flower
from the newly built ruins of the theatre. It is nice to be greeted by
many of the shopkeepers with the Greek for 'Welcome Home'
and the street vendors and tourist touts flatter me by not bothering
me with their spiel. Anyhow many of them are Paxiots and know
me for a poor bit of foreign trash who has settled on their island.

But there is something slightly different about my acquaint-
ances' welcome this year and I cannot help noticing a certain
amount of whispering and pointing going on. Sometimes in
conversation the word 'cinema' occurs and I realize that one of
my old films has been showing in Corfu that winter. One of my
old films. What a pompous phrase! I talk as if I was Miss Alice
Faye or Miss Jessie Matthews. 'One of the films in which I
appeared' is the phrase for which I was searching. Not quite
hard enough as it turned out! Anyhow it was *Doctor Strangelove*
and in the Ionian Bank everyone leaves his place of custom to
shake my hand and explain the plot, my role and the Greek title
of the film, which is all gibberish to me. There is a lot of yelling
and laughing, and casual patrons begin to get alarmed at the
thought of cashing their cheques in such an establishment.

Only Mr Critikos, the manager, who sits at a private table at
the far end of the Bank but completely exposed to the public,

doesn't leave his vulnerable post. He is in the middle of a frantic-ally gesticulating confrontation with some out-of-town farmers, to whom he's trying to impart the Facts of Bank. I have always admired the bravery of Mr Critikos and cannot believe that he isn't occasionally subjected to acts of violence from angry clients. Usually gents in a similar position of power have rooms with glass doors to protect them. But everything about a Greek Bank is more informal than in other countries, though I have no complaints about my English one (Westminster, Sloane Square Branch. Advt). The manager there has been super to me and I only hope he's still there when he reads this. No, seriously, I always expect friendliness from people who look after My Money and not to have my head snapped off every time I pop in and Something Has Gone A Bit Wrong.

That is what I hate about American banks. It's the hypocrisy of the system there which is so deeply revolting. On the one hand they are BEGGING you to borrow from them ('A friendly loan from your friendly bank' is the type of slogan they use *ad nauseam*) and the next moment you are a few dollars overdrawn (even if for one day) and they either have you arrested and/or RD your cheque(s) without referring to you. You are then charged extra for this temporary lapse and treated like a pariah from that moment on. And all because you have been kind enough to lend THEM some money when they probably needed every cent.

I know only too well how they can humiliate you because some beasts called the Scientific Bank Inc. bounced two cheques of mine over the supposedly festive season of Christmas. I had an account with them and had been paying in the residue of my salary from *Luther* every week, and as the show was still a big success it wasn't I thought a wildly 'friendly' gesture from a 'friendly bank' to throw two cheques back in my face, one pay-able to Sardi's Restaurant and the other to St James's Theatre where I had been appearing for some months past. The amount I was overdrawn for twenty-four hours was around the twenty dollar mark. They couldn't have so desperately needed it for Christmas spending could they? Anyhow I was quite cross and the moment I'd righted my balance I left, scattering all those thousands of blank cheques they supply you with all over the floor of dear old Scientific Bank Inc.

Now I have joined the Trade Bank where things are a bit more civilized and the personnel are more personal, though they did suggest at one period that they would like to 'analyse' my account. It was then revealed to me (confidentially of course) that it showed tendencies to erratic behaviour. I could have told them that without putting the poor thing on a couch. Heaven knows what they'd make of the eccentric but delightful behaviour of the staff of the Ionian Bank in Corfu.

So (back in Corfu) I paid in some travellers' cheques when I could get them in edgeways and pressed on to Corfu Travel round the corner. This is an organization with which I have had a good deal of truck over the years. It is run by a saintly but witty lady called Marie Aspioti. She is a member of one of the oldest and most distinguished families in Corfu and received an M.B.E. for work done with the British Council before the Cyprus clash terminated its existence in Greece. A close friend of the Durrells from their arrival in the island in the early thirties, she has kept a gentle but firm hand on Anglo-Hellenic relationships ever since; and now that she has turned her attention to a travel agency you can hear her mollifying many an irate retired colonel who has leased a Corfiote villa from England and arrived to find that half the promised amenities aren't there. This she does in impeccable English (she has for many years taught it in school). She has a large staff who adore her. My particular friend is Hermione of the doe eyes who gives out comfort, ouzo and advice with great sweetness. She telephones me in Paxos and the line is so terrible that neither of us can hear a word the other is saying and we end up with yards and yards of distorted information.

Having caught up with Hermione on Who's Where and With Whom, I think a mid-morning coffee at the Corfu Bar would not come amiss and there I can do a visual check-up. On the way I pass the Aegli Restaurant where the waiters rush me inside to view today's menu and I escape from their clutches and come face to face with the long disconcerting stare of the lady who runs a modern furniture shop and who has been sitting in the window sewing ever since I first clapped eyes on her. I have never seen a customer enter or leave the emporium or one in it and I can only imagine that she deters them by the endless hems she constructs for sheets. Her interest in the outside world appears numbed and I have a feeling she wouldn't flicker an eyelid even if I exposed myself in front of her.

I don't take this extreme step however and round the corner to reach the Parade or Liston as it is called. It is a long series of bars set under a replica (by the same architect) of the Rue de Rivoli. Facing the arcade is a large square, where occasionally cricket is played, a survival from the era of the British Protectorate. There are numerous signs of Anglophilia and, as Mr Durrell has already pointed out in one of his books, the word 'Howzatt' is now part of the Greek language to say nothing of 'Tsintsa Beera'. In spite of Corfu's complete independence I am sure its appeal for British tourists is largely caused by the latent nostalgia for bygone days. A few years back there was a splendid great carry-on to celebrate the centenary of Corfu's freedom from the Protectorate. King Constantine arrived and one of his first official jobs was to open an exhibition of Edward Lear's drawings of the Ionian Islands. Mr Lear lived many years in the city and his diaries of the social life of the period are fascinating.

I don't think a bar in the Old Port called The Spoty Dog was going in those days but there are few corners of the city where there isn't a tiny dash of British flavour. The Corfu Bar is a bit too full of it and at the height of the season it is v. difficult to hear Greek spoken, but the waiters are absolutely splendid and cope inimitably with every type of customer. I order a superior type of ouzo and am brought a selection of mezzay, those delicious hors-d'oeuvres which are always served with this drink. I take a large sip and have a jolly good look-round. With pleasure I note that there is not a single obvious tourist in sight (except perhaps me). But on the other hand there is no sign of the various eccentrics who contribute so much to the Corfiote scene. The locals are by now completely inured to them but to a newcomer they can prove pretty startling.

Where, for instance, is the middle-aged, crippled lady who is dressed and made-up like a lady clown? Carrying enormous earrings and a very elaborate maquillage she looks as if she might start a juggling act any minute. Her story has never been fully explained to me, though I am told on fairly good authority that she enjoys a very happy fantasy life in which she is convinced that every gent whom she meets is besotted forthwith. This would, I suppose, explain her constant darting up and down the streets of an evening to avoid the advances, which she half dreads and half adores.

Then there is the gentleman who forms fours on and off all over the town and has a curious habit of brushing away imaginary flies from his face.

Slightly more sinister is another character with military tendencies. He is very 'with it' sartorially as his accessories are made from leather. He has waistcoats and wristbands of this material and, dangling from one arm, a thonged fly-squatter which he really should lend to the Former of Fours Aforementioned. He has a Nazi haircut and an absolutely square head to go with it. But he has one remarkable and unique achievement to his credit. He did happen to SWIM to Albania. It occurred during the period of tension when in theory it would be easier for me to go through the eye of a needle than for a Corfiote to get into Albania. Even silly but harmless grand yachts tend to get fired on when coasting down from Yugoslavia so it wasn't surprising when the intrepid adventurer found himself clapped into gaol the moment he reached shore. After a summary trial he was apparently released and worked his way through a number of Iron Curtain countries and prisons. I personally can't see how he could have kept his passport dry. He finally reached Turkey and from there it was comparatively plain sailing or swimming. Anyhow he eventually returned to Corfu where he lives with his mother in an oven. You heard! An oven. Disused, as a matter of fact, except by him and even if it was, used I mean, it couldn't have made things much hotter for him than whence he came. And if the grammar and syntax of that sentence haven't made your hair stand on end I'd like to know what would. And I forgot to mention that his mother, as far as one can ascertain, lives perfectly normally in a sitting-room and a bedroom. Once a week she gives him some pocket-money for a 'night-out'. This he spends slowly at the Corfu Bar, drinking in a most sophisticated manner and using the fly-squatter a bit indiscriminately. Most of the time he wears an enigmatic smile, of the type S.S. captains put on during a mass shooting, I imagine, and alarms the nervous passer-by as he carries on an intensive conversation with himself.

Which brings me to Hélène, the district nurse, who recites her own poetry while riding a bicycle or giving injections to patients. After my fourth injection she gave me a bound volume of her collected work, which was entitled *Burning Hearts*. I haven't got very far into the tome but I did for some time carry about with me other examples of her art, notably the crosses with which she marked my body to avoid pricking me in the same spot twice. Marked with a seemingly indelible pencil, I looked like an enormous rather untidy Football Pools Form.

In a different category is the handsome well-born lady, happily married, who outdoes the Mesdames Dietrich, West, Negri, Swanson and Harlow in their palmiest days, with the tightness of her clothes and an outrageously provocative walk. It is reported that whole waves of enthusiastic but mistaken convoys of American sailors follow her everywhere and on one occasion got as far as her private residence. Without looking behind her once, she did then take off her shoes as she opened the door, and throw them with unerring accuracy at the vanguard of her admirers. She is constantly upholstered in either leather or dark satin and, with the highest of heels, dark glasses, and a plethora of veils, has no difficulty in upholding her undoubted position as the Glamour Queen of Uptown Corfu. She is also, I believe, extremely good company.

But, unfortunately, on the morning of my return she is not

there to provide a sight for my sore eyes. I do run into my friend Hector Koliakopolous, however, who is one of the live wires of the town. He, like Marie Aspioti, worked for the British Council and was decorated for it, and speaks very droll but near perfect English. He has written a riveting saga of life in Corfu during the war and has held me enthralled for hours with his stories of the occupation. It is very little-known by the average tourist that the town suffered badly at this period, was roughly handled by Italian and German invaders and bombed appallingly in the process. A year or two ago Hector edited a well-intentioned and mainly English-language newspaper called the *Corfu News*. It failed, principally because the main hotels would not distribute it to their customers as they weren't frightfully keen on any info about 'What's On In Corfu' being conveyed from any other source than their own immensely tippable staffs. The paper was also extremely expensive which may have helped in its demise. I contributed fairly often and submitted a Good Loo Guide for the town and a short but I think effective article on the delights of Paxos, pointing out the difficulties of getting there to taste them.

Hector fills in some gaps by bringing me up to date with the latest Corfiote news and I press on about my business. I glance at the hundreds of tables laid out in the bars both sides of the street (traffic is forbidden here except for prams), but it is too early for the layabouts and new transient hustlers to be having a sitdown. The dear little waiter from the Apollo Bar dashes out and expresses horror that I am monos (alone) and how is the tall dark American I was with last year and will he be back? I give him all the data I want him to hear but realize that I am not holding his entire interest. With an apology he darts away to tempt a couple of nervous American professor-type characters who have obviously arrived in Greece for a cultural but sexy sabbatical, and are at that moment hovering between bars. With a saucy triumphant wink at me, the little waiter lures them to one of his tables by gripping their arms and speaking execrable English. But I still prefer this to the 'Gut Morgen's' I always get from one of the waiters at the next bar who cannot believe that I am not a German. It is my most unfavourite form of address.

It is not used by the taxi-drivers who reside on the crest of the hill which I am now passing. They are lavish in their welcome as I have proved a good customer in the past and now the season is slackish and they spend their time chatting and zizzing in motionless convoy. I proceed along the Promenade, taking a fresh look at the fine old Venetian houses which overlook the Bandstand and the Old Fort. I pass the austere statue of President Capodistria, who appears to be guarding a beautiful bombed-out shell of a house, which has fig-trees sprouting out of the windows.

And on to my most urgent errand which has to be done in the Old Port, where the ferry-boat to Paxos is about to leave. The Old Port is tacky but charming with its sleazy bars and the picturesque Hotel Constantinople. The car-ferry from Igoumenitsa puts in here and most of the small passenger caïques, but big cruising liners and the Brindisi ferry berth at the hideous but commodious New Port.

Today it is the *Aspasia* who is Paxos-bound and I arrive five minutes before its scheduled sailing. Vassilys, the short-sighted first mate, peers for a moment, screams 'Boooly' at me, stops loading drums, and embraces me hotly. He takes my letter announcing my imminent arrival, buries it in his greasy bosom and we can only hope for the best.

The rest of the day is spent in buying household supplies, seeing chums and trying to tire myself out generally so that there is a chance of getting some sleep at night by dulling the excitement which is already surging through me at the thought of The Homecoming.

My tactics succeed and I zizz happily until woken by the museum workers and, after packing and breakfasting in the hotel, a summoned taxi deposits me and an overpowering amount of impedimenta on the jetty. Today it's the turn of the *Epta Nissos* to convey us to Paxos and the fourth mate—about nine years of age, with enormous suitcases under his eyes—handles my ditto with such alarming efficiency that I leave him to get on with it and go off to do last minute shopping in the town. It is quite safe to beetle off because the ship will give a series of ear-splitting blasts before thinking of leaving. So I have plenty of time to get the cold cuts, cheese, fresh veg and fruit which are sometimes scarce in Lakka. I even have time to have a longish session at the well-stocked emporium of Tsirigotis (*Père et Fils*) which has everything from tins of pineapple chunks to Lea and Perrins Worcester sauce, the two comparatively most expensive commodities hereabouts. It always amuses me what chums ask me to bring back from London if I am going there on a brief visit. The luxuries most lusted after are Marmite, Bovril, Golden Syrup and fresh sausages. Chez Tsirigotis, kippers, tea and Catsup are readily obtainable.

I complete my purchases and Père T. gives me a neat brandy which sends me reeling down the street just in time to hear the first warning toot from the *Epta Nissos*. I stagger aboard and make for the top deck which is comparatively empty at this time of year. It is too early in the season for the awning to be up and, as the sun is pretty hot, some of my fellow-passengers are already constructing repellent headgear out of old newspapers. It's all very well for me to jeer and I realize that I shall have to be very careful myself not to burn to a frazzle. The temptation, after months of privation, to expose oneself excessively to the sun is well-nigh irresistible but I know to my cost that an early peeling nose or forehead can wreck weeks of holiday and play havoc with morale.

There is a final hoot to announce our imminent departure and I look over the side to view the last-minute panic. People are streaming across the greensward of the Old Port with letters, fish in newspaper, bits of meat, ice, poultry—live and dead, crates of furniture, and even grandmothers and/or small children to entrust to Marco, the chunky little skipper of the *Epta Nissos*. Neatly dressed businessmen arrive with plastic briefcases, a sailor from the Port Authorities checks in with the sailing orders and complement and then he and we are off.

The first two hours of the voyage, stunning as they are the first time, are now as familiar to me as a routine trip on a number 19 bus from Chelsea to Piccadilly Circus but here for the record are the landmarks which catch the attention cruising down the island of Corfu to its southernmost tip. After rounding the Old Fort and the swanky Corfu Palace Hotel, we get a glimpse through the trees of Mon Repos, the Royal residence where our Prince Philip was born and where the beautiful Queen Anne-Marie of Greece had her baby a few years back. She and her husband often visit the island during the summer months and behave very informally.

We pass Kanoni Point, with its famous view of Mouse Island and the monastery near the causeway, and then Perama, the Tourists' Delight, pops up. With bungalows galore and many restaurants it has become enormously popular though I find its lack of good beaches and its narrow coast roads with the never-ending traffic and screech of brakes anything but relaxing. Beyond Perama and high on the mountain side one can see the extraordinary Achilleon, which was the bizarre baroque and rococo residence of the Kaiser. The gardens stretched right down to the sea and terminated in a terraced bridge where the Kaiserin was wont to stroll up and down. This was bombed during the war and has been left in a state of macabre wreckage though a brand new and rather good Kaiser Bridge Hotel has sprung up alongside. I stayed there for a few days and they hadn't had time to finish the additional floor that they had planned. There was therefore a certain amount of open work and exposure to God's good air going on. The birds however had clocked in as semi-permanent residents and had built nests for themselves in the cisterns of the loos. The management had met them half-way, so to speak, and provided trays on the floor for their convenience.

The Achilleon is now a casino, run by a German concern, where it is also permitted to dine, dance and indeed do a strip-tease or three. The ceilings, statues and paintings suspend belief and the building is well worth a visit. You can reach it through the old and charming village of Gastouri where there are two brothers, both owning grocers' shops on opposite sides of the streets, who haven't addressed a single word to each other in thirty-four years.

Not far from the Achilleon one can clearly make out the new white residence of the lovely gent who has embellished this vol with his drawings. He and his wife Inez live in a simple but very comfortable house, designed by Roger, which stands at the foot of the Manessi property all of which commands a superb view of the sea and the fishing village of Benitsa.

High up stands a big beautiful house called San Stefano, where Mrs Manessi plays hostess to so many distinguished foreign visitors and Greek notables; it has a wonderful atmosphere. The chatelaine has watched with pride the astonishing industry and resulting success of her three sons: George and Theodore run the biggest garage and car-hire service in Corfu and Stephen husbands the vast olive acreage. All the Manessis speak impeccable English and their kindness to my fellow-countrymen is legendary.

Benitsa itself is a rapidly expanding tourist centre. There is for me rather too prevalent a pong of fish to attract me as a resident, but the cosy Avra Hotel, run by two English-speaking brothers, and a number of simple but good restaurants, including the Fresh Fish (Psaria Fresca), draw the tourists; and the bathing, though by no means perfect, is much better than at Perama.

After skirting Benitsa there is about an hour of very flat land to watch or skip watching. We pass the almost hidden river mouth which leads to Lefkimmi, the industrial centre of the south, and stop at Cavos a few miles further on, where we had that notable lobster tuck-in. This visit we stay briefly to take on a few passengers, and are now all set for the last lap. In a few minutes we will have passed the tip of Corfu and be crossing the channel between the two islands. The sea is quite calm, which is more than I am. I know full well that it is only a short time before I can actually see To Spiti Mou. I pretend to be non-chalant about the whole thing but I notice that the crew of the

Epta Nissos are watching my reactions with interest. So when eventually the tiny white shape is visible they gather round me exclaiming 'Tee aurea!' (How beautiful!). And of course they are right. It is beautiful. Soon I can make out the green shutters and doors, the white walls and—hey! what's that? Something fluttering in the wind. It's the Greek flag to welcome me back. Alekkos has gone too far, I think, as I brush away a not remotely furtive tear. It's all strong emotional stuff and why the hell not? This is what I've been dreaming of on and off since I was last here. In dressing-rooms and hotel bedrooms both sides of the Atlantic there has been a snap of what I am looking at this very moment, and whenever I have been particularly exasperated or unhappy over a chore I have just reassured myself as to exactly what I'm working for. And the answer is quite simple. It's for that funny squat building in Paxos and to give her all the things that might make her happier inside AND out.

For the umpteenth time I wonder how she can remain balanced so perilously on the cliff's edge and not slide into Hee Thalassa. I can't quite make out To Sterna on which I've pinned so many hygienic hopes. I am glad of this because with luck it is totally concealed behind My Olives; a Good Thing, as it is unlikely to be of great beauty. But that anyhow is the last quality I want in my sterna. I would like total reliability and dependaditto, two rare attributes in inanimate objects around this area.

We are now gliding into the little harbour of Lakka and I am relieved to notice at first glance that nothing has changed. There are the two biggish caïques, deserted as usual and at anchor. They appear hardly ever to leave port and I wish they would present me with one to go pottering round the islands in. Over on the left by the schoolhouse are the two halves of the broken wreck which no one has ever bothered to remove. I notice that the water in the inner port is dark brown, stained by the olive-press reject stuff. This happens every second year and is one of the reasons why I have arrived a little later this time. As I have stated earlier the entire island is given over to the gathering and pressing of the fruit and a curiously sickly smell pervades the air round the port. I can hear the presses whirring away though we are several yards from the jetty, but what is really worrying me is the fact that I can't see a single soul waiting to greet me or indeed any of the other passengers. It was all very different when I left them, I think to myself in an orgy of self-pity. The whole village turned out for that one.

After all I have given them due warning of my approach, via Alekkos, and at least he might have turned up to give me a hand with the luggage. But I haven't allowed for the fact that the *Epta Nissos* has done the journey from Corfu in near record time (just over three hours) and we have caught the village off its guard. However a toot from the ship brings them scurrying from every direction, crying-out, waving and carrying-on generally in a deeply moving fashion. As we start securing to the jetty the air is filled with shouts of 'Kyrios Bull' or 'Booooly'. Figures detach themselves from the general melée and Dmitri, the Priest's son, is first aboard. He gives me a rose, grabs my luggage and disappears over the side in a flash. I pass the more fragile stuff through the porthole to Alekkos, who is on shore with his son Giovanni (Yannis). This gets rid of the typewriter, the filter pump and a string bag jammed with string beans. I jump ashore and hug everyone in sight. They all start yelling at me and it is bedlam. It takes me a long time to understand what they are trying to tell me, which is that Mr Ypsilos is in Corfu and I've just missed him by a day. This leads up to the Village Joke, which is Me Overacting Grief at his absence. I'm afraid I have a big personal success with my performance and I have to Keep It Up for a bit. However Spiro Café leads the way to his establishment where we sit down and have a turcico.

But both he and Alekkos have registered my ill-concealed impatience to get to To Spiti Mou and we are soon on our way, the 'we' now including the two mules who have joined us and on which Apergis Senior and Junior mount themselves. I follow at a discreet distance to avoid any misadventure and, rounding the corner by the abattoir, we run slap into the entire village school, just dismissed. They send up cheers and hoots. They also

say 'Kerete' about eighty-five times. ('Welcome', 'Hallo' or 'Goodbye', according to circumstances. That's what's so hair-raising about the Greek language!) I am rather glad of this diversion because it is better to get the reunion over this way and not celebrate it by distracting the children in the middle of a class when I pass their open window on the way to the village. They usually react rather too strongly to this and I can't always remember to duck my head to avoid being seen.

My encounter with the children also means that I can stop looking at the water in the inner harbour, which is quite wildly unattractive at this time of year, not only steeped in olive-residue but laced with a sprinkling of dead cats and birds, to say nothing of the odd reject from the abattoir down the road. I have arrived in the middle of the shooting season when the whole of the island go mad about the trigonia, a small quail-like chap who settles briefly but unwisely on Paxos, which appears to be on his migrating route. They come in their thousands and the inhabitants treat them like dangerous criminals. The air is horrendous with the sound of gunshot and many's the guest who has had the bejesus scared out of him as a bullet or a bit of flying shrapnel goes whizzing past his head.

If they, the house guests, have been having a bit of a zizz on the terrace they tend to complain. 'Oh, it's only the trigonia,' I say irritably and go about my business as if it was the most natural thing in the world; I hear them muttering about Cyprus and/or the Blitz, and I do have to admit that there have been some close shaves. It's the silliness of the birds that upsets me so. You would have thought by now the word would have got round and they would have got visas for some other island, where possibly the inhabitants wouldn't all be lying in wait. I find myself longing for winds and bad weather so that at any rate one doesn't hear the gunfire. I rarely catch sight of the unknown assailants but I am often the recipient of their prey. Alekkos is constantly bringing me up specimens, pre-cooked in a delicious sauce by Mrs Alekkos, and I have to confess that I don't throw them in his face, because they are tasty, to put it mildly, and make a change from the perpetual buck rarebits I construct for myself when I'm alone.

But when the trigonia are slit down the middle and given to me raw, with their tiny organs showing, it's throw-up time as far as I'm concerned and supperless to bed, Master Peter, if necessary. Well that's enough of that, but thousands of them do fall in the sea and I hate seeing them floating about in the harbour before being eaten by the fish.

On to To Spiti Mou however. We pass the schoolhouse and greet Ho Didaskalos (The Schoolmaster) who is clearing up, and we are all set for the steep path up the cliff. It's not very sunny so the ascent isn't as breath-taking (in the strict sense of the word) as it can be. I look busily for landmarks and they aren't hard to find. By now the open sea is below us and I notice that the little channel I made through the rocks last year, to make bathing easier, is still just chartable, though I shall have to do some serious work on it later. At the moment the water will be far too cold to permit a long wallow in it and it won't really be warm until the beginning of June. The way up seems more stony and undisciplined than ever and I stumble many times. In a few days I shall have got back into the rhythm of the thing and be walking as delicately and as surely as an elephant. What, didn't you know about elephants walking delicately? I always think of a film called *Elephant Walk* in this connection. One of the main scenes was of a stampede by the animals through the house that Miss Elizabeth Taylor lived in. Technicians had built an exact replica of the interiors in papier mâché so that the slightest touch would crush and crumple furniture, walls and indeed the entire building. Came the day for shooting this destruction. The elephants were lined up, the word 'Action' was given by the director, great thwacks were administered to the dear animals' behinds and off they trotted, only to pick their way so gently and perceptively that not one article in any of the sets was as much as grazed. Everyone was LIVID.

Which theatrical anecdote has damn all to do with my return to The Bullings as I have never seen an elephant on Paxos personally, but I suppose I hoped that it might break the already near-nauseating nostalgic flavour of these recollections. Ah, here is the rock where N. used to sit sketching the little town. The paint stains are clearly visible and, goodness, what bright colours! Yellow, red and turquoise to capture that astonishing liquid below. On the next bend I recall a misguided attempt of mine to take a short cut late at night, which landed me flat on the stony ground with multiple cuts and literally egg on my face, as I was carrying eggs at the time. And here is the little grove where a French couple were at it like knives from the moment the ferry-boat arrived from Gaios in the morning until another took them back in the late afternoon. I presume they never let up, as I had to make rather a lot of business trips to the village that day and there didn't seem much change in the general position. I didn't like to ask them in for a nice cup of tea or a chat or something as the poor dears obviously thought they were invisible to passing traffic in mules or people.

And now we have reached the top and there is only the narrow path leading to the house to be negotiated. Bushes each side touch one's typewriter and filter pump but I've never bothered to trim them, acting on the theory that the very density of 'The Drive' will deter all but the most tenacious of intruders. Actually the path is 'right of way' but very few of the locals seem to want to exercise it and I must say here and now that I am deeply grateful for their respect for my privacy.

And now the great moment of truth has arrived. I stop for a split second by the grey side wall (now white, thanks to D.N.'s industry) and I am shaking with excitement. When I get round to the front will it be exactly as I remember it? Since I left last July how many times, in moments of stress and unhappiness, I have been able to close my eyes and project the house on a private screen inside my head. Supposing it's totally different? Supposing somebody has altered it all and put a thatched roof on it and stone dwarfs on the terrace? Can the Irish Adventurer whom I left as housekeeper have turned the whole thing into a racing stable and imported a bog in addition, to make him feel at home? Perhaps it was a mistake to send him out all those copies of *Horse and Hound* and *Stud and Stable*. No I'm being silly, I know, because there'd be a fat chance of him turning it into a bog, with all that lack of water.

I slither round the corner and get my first pleasant surprise. The vine is growing slowly up the side of the house. I say 'the' vine because the other three have vanished into the ground or down the goats' tums like greased lightning. To my delight the front of the house is very white and Alekkos tells me that the Irish A. did this just before leaving. That was nice of him, but I do wish he hadn't borrowed my binoculars (this I discover a few hours later) and left his weights in exchange (presumably). And I don't mean the English cigarettes of that name. He did hitch-hike with them across Europe, which is the sort of spookily endearing thing that the Irish A. tends to do.

I remember his arrival on the island one year when I was frightfully cross with him about something or other and I didn't give him the warm welcome he was expecting. In fact, as the ferry-boat clocked in and I saw his bearded face in the prow, I waved lazily in reply to his greeting and continued to lie on the beach nonchalantly. Eventually he came round from the harbour, carrying a couple of suitcases, and I felt a bit ashamed of my Instant Churl, as Elliott Reid, the American actor, would say. And has. Constantly. To our pleasure. Anyhow I offered Instant Help to the Irish A., by offering to help him with his luggage up the hill. He quickly handed me one of his suitcases and I fell to the ground under the weight or, as it turned out, the weights with which he had crammed the damned thing. It was too late in the day to throw him and/or his weights into the Ionian and a few hours later we were having a nice cup of tea and happily playing chess. Well, not happily perhaps, speaking for myself, because I was being beaten. One of the more curious complications about my relationship with the Irish Adventurer is the fact that I simply will not admit that someone who appears to be not frightfully good at Lifemanship can be better than I at a game like chess. As you see, I'm not likely ever to clothe myself in

Instant Humility. I could cope with him winning at Poker, Monopoly or Beggar-my-Neighbour but then they are largely luck. His skill and arrogance at chess drive me up the wall or usually straight into the sea. Not that he always wins but consistently enough to make me want to beat the daylights out of him at Scrabble. This is comparatively easy because he spells even worse than I. Though I am now slightly chary of playing any new game with him as he always pretends that he has never had a go at it.

But I know that it's fairly impossible to be surprised by anything that the Irish A. does or knows. In his twenty-seven extremely odd years he has done practically everything which should qualify him for immediate serialization in the *News of the W*. He has, for instance, been a professional poker-player in Peru, a masseur in Rome, a racehorse-owner in Madrid, a restaurateur in Putney, a commissionaire for a Soho strip-club and a fairly continuously employed stunt man for many famous epics. Falling over cliffs on horses, blowing up bridges, and being crucified or burned at the stake are old hat to him, so in some ways he should make an admirable housekeeper for a small house on a remote Greek island. He has also starved from Segovia to Southfields and so is fairly adaptable to thick and thin. And that's enough about the Irish Adventurer, who may very easily either be in the Foreign Legion or running a boutique at this very moment. Or, come to think of it, living in To Spiti Mou.

Anyhow, apart from the whitewashed walls, weights and *Horse and Hound*, there is little trace of him today and, as ever, the interior is miraculously unchanged and so clean and fresh that I embrace the front door and Alekkos, neither of whom is remotely embarrassed. I have a brief look at the shelves which are as complete and comprehensive as I reported at the beginning of this chapter. One or two strange phenomena have survived the interim period. The glass which used to serve as the Wasps' Torture Chamber is still half-filled with water and honey, a mixture which used to drive the little beasts out of their minds as they fell in and couldn't climb out again. Because I was jolly

well there to see that they didn't. I used to watch their frenzied
efforts with huge sadistic pleasure, partic after having been stung
by one which flew into my mouth while I was eating a Jumbo
Pork Luncheon Meat Sandwich. It struck just as the *Epta Nissos*,
with me as a passenger, was slipping out of Corfu. By the time
we docked at Lakka my cheek had swollen up like a balloon and
I explained to the ever-inquisitive Mr Ypsilos that I had got my
wound from fighting in Albania. But it's curious how one can't
keep one's mouth open if a wasp flies in. If one could, it would
enable the bloody thing to take one look inside and fly out again.
But oh no, one has to snap one's great silly jaws together and no
wonder the animal gets into a tizzy and stings one.

Today there are no customers for the Wasps' Torture Chamber
but the glass brings back happy if macabre memories. The
Colman's mustard powder has gone a v. funny colour but, to
compensate, the tin of Nescafé seems almost pristine in Instant
Flavour. Everything else is more than O.K. and I turn my
attention to the permanent fixtures. The cracks in the hand-basin
are no worse, the loo is quite its post-being-blessed self, and,
after a little coaxing, the refrigerator is responding in its cold way.

'Tora To Sterna,' (And now the Water-Cistern) says Alekkos
bringing me up with a bump.

We go out to inspect This Year's Improvement and it is
obvious from the word Go that It is This Year's Disappointment.
It is a hideous, squat grey building, looking like a gun emplace-
ment without guns. But perhaps it will eventually serve its
purpose if we can just find the means of extracting the vast
reserves of water which I've gone to such enormous expense to
get imprisoned there. At the moment there is only a tiny spas-
modic trickle through the midget tap which has been affixed to
the base of the huge edifice. Even Alekkos is a tidge disturbed
as he bangs away with a pair of pliers. It is typical, I fear, of Greek
workmanship that To Sterna, which cost almost as much as the
original house, is as yet almost totally useless. Later I discover
that all the gutters on the roof, which were meant to convey the
rainwater, are riddled with holes like Gruyère cheese. This

accounts for the few inches of water which repose at the bottom of To Sterna and might last us three weeks if we are economical. I have by this time got on top of the beast and lowered a bamboo pole to assess the treasure. Part of the trouble was caused by Nikos's mishap before its completion; I know he would have made it work somehow but in my experience mechanical or non-totally essential jobs are almost always disasters, I find, and I still can't quite understand why the lavatory cannot swallow any kind of paper. This is the case with loos all over Greece and leads to the use of those wildly attractive wastepaper baskets where one deposits the end product, if I may use the phrase.

Alekkos is a bit subdued by the obvious disappointment I show over To Sterna but I reassure him of my gratitude for his guarding my property so beautifully, press a half-bottle of whisky into his hands and give young Yannis a very elaborate pencil which has twelve colours to choose from. Later, in Corfu, I see the same article but of slightly superior quality. The pair depart on their mules and I am left Master of All I Survey, except perhaps To Sterna which I will attempt to blot out of my mind.

I start with a jolly good look-round. I don't need an inventory or library catalogue. There on the bookshelves are most of my favourite books. Practically everything Evelyn Waugh ever wrote, some E. M. Forster, P. G. Wodehouse and the Somerset Maugham *Short Stories*. A year of rather damp *Paris Match* completes the available reading material but there is always the Jackson Pollock jigsaw, guaranteed to send any guest out of his or her mind, even if there are no pieces missing. And there is the chess set, scene of so many bitter battles and the Travel Scrabble, worn and scarred, with all the tiles gathered together in a smelly old washing-bag. There is a battered set of patience cards, their faces worn away during evenings of loneliness and unhappiness. I know this last sentence may surprise you and I hasten to add that the evenings in question were few in number but here is the most suitable moment to make a confession. I am nowhere near as self-contained as I thought I was and after a few days in the house on my own I get edgy and totally disenchanted.

Part of it is the language situation, and the moment I get more fluent I can do some intelligent entertaining and not just trot out phrase-book clichés. But I am as yet the only foreigner on the island, as far as I know, so there are stretches of silence to which I'm not used.

The flow of guests has been constant and stimulating to a degree. I find that Paxos has a quite extraordinary effect on most visitors: they blossom and take on the magic with which the island seems to be sprinkled. Relationships have bloomed and the customers always appear to want to return. For me the ideal spacing is to have about three days between visitors so as to tart the place up a bit and get some stocks of food and wine in.

At this very moment of my homecoming, though, I am blissfully happy to be alone, safe in the knowledge that a whole series of delightful persons are scheduled to visit me, and I continue my tour of inspection of the premises in a state of contentment. The old lares and penates are disclosed one after the other, as here I have been able to indulge to excess my penchant for hoarding. There is room for the wildest of whims. In the loo is a fishing-net I bought the first year and haven't used since. I was informed by Nikos that the dear little fish wouldn't dream of going anywhere near white nylon, which it is made of. It's not worth dyeing at this late date, if you know what I mean. I remember dragging it along the bottom of the sea with no success of any sort. It is particularly humiliating when one can see shoals of the little dears whizzing happily by, cocking piscine snooks at one. They are very cheeky indeed round here and pop in between one's toes without so much as a by your leave.

On to the medicine shelf and it is always comforting to find it so healthily stocked. The Meggazones, mind you, have taken a bit of a beating and turned into globules of stickiness but the Nippon Ant Poison is intact as are the Flying-Bomb AND the Bam-Bum Fly-dispatchers. I see also Dr Debat's Poudre Inctyol, but this provides a mystery, as eczema, for which the good medico has concocted a remedy, is one of the few diseases, touch olives, that hasn't come my way. As yet.

Which brings us to the entire medical problem affecting the inhabitants of Paxos. The doctor, who is delightful, lives some five miles away from our village and about a mile out of Gaios. He is therefore not all that accessible and, having no transport of his own, it doesn't make his or the ailing person's predicament an easy one. I am sure that in extreme emergency a message would be got to him somehow, but usually it's a question of taking up one's bed and walking, or sometimes with luck taking up somebody else's bus: The Two Brothers, as a matter of fact, that friendly vehicle whose character I have already discussed at length in an earlier and possibly less boring chapter. Certainly a shorter one. Will it never end? Yes. Anyhow The Two Brothers clocks out at seven in the morning from downtown Lakka and one descends at the doctor's pretty surgery some twenty minutes later. One may wait anything up to two hours for his advent. The whole procedure differs somewhat from what goes on in the National Health Service but then on the other hand quite a percentage of the gents who work under that organization would not (a) give their male patients a camellia or two before examination or (b) bring in their wives and/or secretaries to have a jolly good look at the patients during it (the examination I mean).

Quite apart from the camellias and assorted cuttings my Greek doctor gives me, he also has a plentiful supply of penicillin and a good many modern appliances. He is courteous, brisk and professional and I have every confidence in his ability. I just wish it wasn't so difficult to get hold of him. The solution is, of course, to fall ill on a Wednesday because that is the day he visits Lakka. He arrives on the morning ferry-boat around ten and takes surgery in the harbour master's office but I get embarrassed going there because all the other patients insist on my jumping the queue. The stranger always come first on Greek islands and I have known elderly ladies on buses try to get me to take their seats, if you know what I mean.

If one has had to go to Gaios to see the doctor and he has dealt with one's complaint(s) quickly enough, one is faced with a semi-trot down the hill to arrive in time to catch the early ferry-boat back to Lakka. Once I was lucky enough to catch the skipper of same (Mitsos of The Pullman) on his motor-bike on his way to the port, and pretty bizarre I looked and felt on his pillion. But this was a freak of chance and one cannot be ill AND better to order. If the doctor takes a long time over deciding on the complaint and the cure, there is no hope of returning home until late in the evening, unless one cares to walk to Magazia (just the four miles, thank you very much, and not a frightfully attractive proposition if one happens to have a poisoned foot). But there is no doubt that one feels much better after a visit to the 'giatros' (doctor). This curious fact is due, I imagine, partly to the dread of having to go through the ordeal again. In fairness to the system it must be admitted that the doctor does cover all the remoter parts of the island during the week, mainly on foot.

One day he will be presented with a car or at least a Vespa but at present there are remarkably few vehicles on the island. Lorries and vans are in adequate supply but a private car is a rarity, as it is etsi-ketsi getting one on the ferry-boat. We do however have traffic problems and it would help enormously if the hundreds of mules who serve as transport had tail-lamps or number plates or something.

I leave the medicine shelf reluctantly. This year I'll try not to poison my ear or leg and keep healthy all the time. I go outside and breathe long and deeply the cool rich air. All the chairs are set on the terrace and I test them all for strength. Then I walk round my estate and inspect the ant situation. Tomorrow I'll join battle with them. They appear to love the Nippon Ant Poison, which isn't very satisfactory.

After a cup of tea I unpack before setting forth for the village to make my bows. It is easy, with no immediately expected guest, to stow everything away tidily and calmly and soon I am on the down path, so to speak, dressed in a newish wardrobe to indicate the Importance of the Occasion. Tomorrow it'll be back to the sloppy worn clothes which they know backwards and which indeed look as if I'd put them on backwards.

I go from shop to shop, making tiny speeches about how happy I am to be back home. I am given a touching welcome, most of the shopkeepers offer me an ouzaki (small ouzo) and the grocer gives me two lettuces instead of one. The trickiest gift is from Nikolaus, who owns the bar opposite Spiro Theophrastus's café. It consists of two raw trigonia, with their poor little guts slit up the middle. He pops them into some bits of newspaper through which the blood seeps instantly and I have difficulty in keeping the package away from the lovely Greek youhourti (yogurt) I have stocked up with.

I visit every shop in the village. Last year Nikos the Fissesman said to me:

'Mr Peetsa, everyone love you in Lakka Paxos, but could you go not always to small shops but to all. Then everyone happy.' Which means distributing my purchases over the widest area, but, as nearly every store sells exactly the same type of goods, it means a great deal of ingenuity to keep trade in circulation. Last year (a non-olive producing one) I did get the feeling that I was one of the few strictly cash customers around.

Alekkos has accompanied me on my rounds, and at the foot of the hill I bid him good night, telling him once again of my happiness and gratitude to the village for being so super to me. This doesn't prevent me from flinging the blood-soaked package into the sea half-way up the hill and giving the trigonia a decent but watery burial.

When I finally reach To Spiti Mou it is sunset-time and I lower the flag. I look out and down on what to me is the most beautiful view in the world. I turn to the house and am deeply moved by what I see. Quite suddenly I wish that all the people I love most in the world could be standing there with me, sharing the magic of a dream come true.

Postscript

It must be admitted that my first intention on writing this delightfully illustrated but haphazard book was to leave out the name of the island on which To Spiti Mou stands. Up till now I have kept it all pretty quiet, as far as the general public is concerned, and evaded the issue by quite nauseating displays of coyness. In fact on television on both sides of the Atlantic, phrases like 'an island whose name I've forgotten' have passed my lips.

The problems of discovering a 'hide-out' are twofold. On the one hand one is dying to show off one's perception and cleverness and, on the other, one is trying to prevent other persons going there. The moment dear witty lamented Nancy Spain mentioned the island of Sciathos in 'The News of the Woggers', the price of land rocketed up and a great many people made a bee-line for it on their next holiday, having never previously heard of the place. It is obvious to me that the news-paper public is avid for suggestions and will react as strongly to an article as they do to an effective advertising campaign. I know this very well because of an article I wrote in the *Sunday Express* about Corfu some years ago. I was asked to write about Paxos but settled for the larger island as I thought I could do some of the smaller establishments a bit of good. Also the money was jolly d. Anyhow the flood of letters I got in absolutely astounded me. Quite a few people announced that they were packing everything up and going to live on Corfu for the rest of their lives. These I had to answer, trying to deter them from doing anything quite so drastic. Some I even met because I got such a guilt complex about my catalysis. The ones who thought I was the travel expert on the newspaper and asked me about Morocco and Manila I ignored. But the power of the press was clearly indicated to me yet again.

I am hoping that the difference between spotlighting a particular place in a national paper and a book is as large as I believe it to be. To my horror, Miss Spain in her last book drew attention to Paxos as being my 'away from it all' habitat. Yet the little island has not been flooded with tourists, trippers and would-be land-owners. Of course mentioning ME by name may have put them off. I hadn't thought of that. But I do remember going to desperate lengths to ensure privacy a few years back. I was over in Corfu and ran into a lady I know who writes travel pieces for all the most chic glossy magazines. She was hot feet from the opening of the Athens Hilton and thirsty for information about Corfu or indeed anything. I told her about the crème caramel at Costas Hotel and one or two other obscure and insufficiently publicized delights of the island.

After I'd finished and she'd taken a notette or three, she said: 'Tomorrow I'm going to what I'm told is the most beautiful island in Greece.'

I gripped the sides of the chair in the café where we were quaffing a delicious apricot drink (Rikofix).

'Which one?' I asked.

'Paxos.'

'Oh,' I said in what I hoped was my best casual disinterested voice.

'Have you been there?' she asked.

'Oh yes, indeed.'

'What's it like?'

'Frightful,' I heard myself saying. 'Very rocky and forbidding. Nothing at all to do.'

'Oh,' said this lady, 'I heard it was quite lovely and totally unspoilt.'

'Unspoilt, you say? Yes, that's possibly true. But only because of the behaviour of the Paxiots,' I said.

'What do you mean?' Milady was wide-eyed.

'Well,' I replied, warming to my subject. 'They're a bit off. They are the only unfriendly Greeks I've ever met. Did you see *Zorba the Greek?*'

'Yes.'

'Well, you remember the scene where they throw stones at that pretty lady with the black hair? It's all a bit like that. They actually hit me twice.' And I pointed at two cuts on my leg which I received at Littlehampton at the age of six from my brother having a bit of a bash at me with a spade.

'Oh dear,' said the travel expert. 'You do depress me. But I think I've got to go. Somebody has laid on a special boat.'

And that was that.

After buying her some pistachio nuts that she fancied (not much use as ammunition against the Paxiots I warned her) I gloomily left her. I ran into some Greek friends of mine who were fully cognizant of my views about publicizing the island. I told them of the sense of doom I felt. They suggested that the only thing to do was to invoke the help of St Spiridion. This I did, and the next day a super gale came whirring up, which made the lady's passage impossible, if you know what I mean. But of course I (or indeed St S.) could not keep it up indefinitely and she eventually got to Paxos. But the small paragraph she wrote extolling its charms was hidden so securely in the magazine that I doubt if it did serious damage.

The next shock to my system was when I was asked to contribute an article about Paxos to the *Corfu News*, a sheet to cater mainly for the tourist.

'Are you mad?' I asked the editor who happened to be a chum.

He smiled at me quizzically and shrugged I think it was his shoulders.

A few weeks later he confronted me again. This time it was serious.

'I have to warn you,' he announced, 'that we are publishing something about Paxos in the next few weeks, whether you write it or not.'

It ended in me writing it because I conceitedly calculated that I could soften any impact by attempting to appeal only to the off-beat traveller. I wrote realistically and quite truthfully about the snags in getting there and finding accommodation, and the general lack of tourist facilities.

I went back to Paxos a bit disturbed. On the way over I realized that it was only a question of postponing the inevitable. I travelled with one of the most distinguished people on the island and he told me that they were expecting sixty journalists from the mainland during the week and asked would I, as the only foreigner living on the island, come and tell them how lovely it all was.

I couldn't say no. And, though—without even praying to St Spiridion this time—bad weather stopped this fresh danger it made me think very seriously about the island and my friends the islanders. It was obviously useless and perhaps wicked to stop any flow of tourist trade, which Paxos needs so desperately. It's a rich island in many ways but, apart from the olives, business is incredibly static and the shops appear to exist mainly on credit. There is little stimulus to enlarge their stock or keep a wider variety and what restaurants there are cater for the residents and are not very flexible in their menus. Yachts tend to press on to Corfu in spite of the bathing and the beauty of the smaller island. There is a trickle of adventurous tourists to the capital but apart from the skin-diving section of the Club Mediterranée there are rarely any foreigners around. The younger generation tend to drift off to find excitement elsewhere, though Paxiots who have lived in America or on the mainland all their lives seem to return to their birthplace for their last span of life.

I want it both ways. I want Paxos to have prosperity and yet remain totally unspoilt. This is, I know, impossible. And it is no good pretending that anything I can do will stop Paxos becoming a Greek St Tropez if that's the way the cookie crumbles. I have seen it happen also with most unlikely Spanish villages, and Ibiza and Ischia are not exactly as they were a couple of decades ago.

So, while I privately want to keep everything exactly the same, it is a selfish wish, I know. If on reading this book of mine you feel that you would like to see for yourselves what Paxos is really like, please pay no attention to me. You will find her people quite exceptional in their simplicity and openness and above all in their love for the stranger. They have welcomed me with unquestioning hearts and made me feel part of them. They will do the same for you. All I ask of you is that you fit in with their way of life and do not expect them to fit in with yours. They were there before you and they know what it's all about.

Life I mean.

F. Harry Stowe.

Lakka,
Paxos.

Hollywood,
California.

Lightning Source UK Ltd.
Milton Keynes UK
UKHW041256040219
336707UK00001B/100/P